AF386177

Murder on Iona

Murder on Iona

The Strange and Mysterious Death of Norah Fornario

Neil R. Storey

First published in Great Britain in 2026 by
Pen & Sword History
An imprint of Pen & Sword Books Limited
Yorkshire – Philadelphia

ISBN 978 1 03614 539 2

A CIP catalogue record for this book is
available from the British Library.

Typeset by Mac Style
Printed in the UK by CPI Group (UK) Ltd, Croydon, CR0 4YY.

The Publisher's authorised representative in the EU for product
safety is Authorised Rep Compliance Ltd., Ground Floor,
71 Lower Baggot Street, Dublin D02 P593, Ireland.
www.arccompliance.com

For a complete list of Pen & Sword titles please contact

PEN & SWORD BOOKS LIMITED
47 Church Street, Barnsley, South Yorkshire, S70 2AS, England
E-mail: enquiries@pen-and-sword.co.uk
Website: www.pen-and-sword.co.uk
or
PEN AND SWORD BOOKS
1950 Lawrence Road, Havertown, PA 19083, USA
E-mail: uspen-and-sword@casematepublishers.com
Website: www.penandswordbooks.com

*This book is dedicated to the memory of
Marie Edith Emily Norah Fornario (1896–1929)*

Contents

Introduction

It is very necessary with so much occult knowledge about, that people should know an occult attack when they see it. These things are much more common than is generally realised. The recent tragedy in Iona gives point to this assertion. No occultist is under any illusion as to that death being from natural causes.

Dion Fortune

No truer words could be said of the Hebridean island of Iona in the 1920s than to describe it as remote. Located over 45 miles to the west of the Scottish mainland, it would take a train journey, a ferry, the crossing of the Island of Mull by horse and cart, bus or car and another ferry from Mull to Iona to get there. Iona had no major roads, no electricity, running water, street lamps, daily papers (there were newspapers, but they usually arrived a day behind) or telephones. Still, it drew many visitors who came to see the ruins and restoration of its religious houses because of their connection to St Columba, the man credited with bringing Christianity to Scotland. With its wide-open skies, fresh sea air and the escape it offered from the hustle and bustle of the mainland Iona was a place of pilgrimage, spirituality and tranquillity, and remains so. Those who lived on the island seemed quite content to do so; most had been born and raised there as their ancestors had been for generations before. It was all they knew. The island of Iona was owned by successive Dukes of Argyll; there was no overlord resident on the island and no great estate there where many locals were in the employ of the laird. Every local on Iona was pretty much the same class. Islanders turned their hand to fishing and agriculture to put food on their tables and earn a living or had skills in trades useful to fellow islanders. Some rowed visitors in and out from the steamers that brought them, while others made and sold items to the visitors or leased out their spare rooms to those who wished to stay overnight, for a week or even a season. The highlights of life for the people of Iona were very much simple pleasures; there were gatherings for traditional dancing, clan gatherings, competitive playing of the bagpipes, highland games and an annual Highland Games on Mull.

Above all, most Iona residents chose to live their own lives without too much outside interference. Some of them were still known to spend most of their lives on the island with only the occasional trip across to Mull and never set foot on mainland Scotland, let alone visited one of its cities. Many islanders were wary of more urban areas and would try to avoid visiting them. Those making any visits would be advised to be very cautious. Even walking around urban areas was a concern for those used to living in such a rural environment. The *Oban Times* even printed reminders of the dangers faced by those crossing roads in towns with such features as 'The Kerb Step', which explained there are 118 pedestrians killed every week and 3,179 injured in mainland road accidents every week and offered the step-by-step method of: 'When crossing the street bring both feet to rest on the kerb (that induces immediate concentration). Look right. Look Left. All Clear. Step off.'[1]

Sundays were kept sacred. In 1928, the opening of tea rooms at Ganavan on a Sunday had been hotly debated by Oban Town Council. During that debate, it was even suggested that the hiring out of seaside bathing boxes should not be permitted. Provost MacArthur moved that bathing boxes be closed, along with the pavilion, on Sundays. He considered that 'there was just as much harm letting the bathing boxes as there was serving tea'. Councillor Livingstone seconded the Provost's notion and made the point, 'if they were to permit one refreshment place to open, they might as well allow the whole lot to do so. They had no right to trifle with the Sunday; it was their duty to support everything that tended to conserve Sunday for the purpose for which it was instituted.'[2]

In 1929, there was no permanent police presence on Iona; in fact, there never had been and the situation has not changed to this day. If police were required they would called in from the neighbouring larger island of Mull where there was the Mull Police Division that consisted of a total of one Inspector, four Sergeants and twenty Constables working out of

1. *Oban Times*, 1 March 1930
2. *Oban Times*, 18 February 1928

three police stations situated at Tobermory, Bunessan and Salen (today there is a fourth police station at Craignure).

The police of Mull Division were pretty much left to their own devices with only occasional inspections carried out by HM Inspector of Constabulary for Scotland. Today, there are just seven police officers on Mull; if a call is made for police assistance, it goes through to Oban and they decide which off-duty police officer should be assigned to deal with it.

The crime rate in the islands was negligible and those who served on the Mull force back in 1929 were very much the sort of officers that just wanted to get on with their jobs with as little hassle as possible and have a quiet life. The difficult terrain and many unmade roads seriously limited the use of any motorised vehicles, so police patrols were carried out on foot and horseback. Most of the islanders spoke Gaelic and preferred to do so even if they could speak English too. Any police officer who was not able to speak Gaelic would soon be found out and would be at a severe disadvantage because of the language barrier.

The Argyll Police Report was published with some pride each year in the local press and gives a real insight into just how little disruption there was to law and order in the rural areas islands:

Chief Constable's report always issued with admirable promptitude, show an increase of 206 crimes and offences reported to the police of the county in 1927, but none in the total of 1429 was of a serious nature. The country districts are singularly free from offences.

Blairmore and Lochaline stations had a clean sheet and Kinlochleven only reported half the offences of the previous year, which amount to one a month.

The percentage of those apprehended while more or less under the influence of drink, shows a gratifying decrease. In 1926 it amounted to 31 percent but in 1927 to only 21 per cent. The nuisance of vagrants seems incurable, for in the double census for the year past they numbered 413 which is an increase of 30 over the previous year.

On the preventative side, which the police make now as important as their criminal work which involves much unseen labour, information was given in 1303 cases to the parties concerned that their premises were insecure during the night, over a million sheep were dipped under their supervision, 68 stray dogs were apprehended, 24 dogs implicated in sheep worrying were traced and destroyed, 413 articles lost were restored to their owners and the kindly offices of the police force sheltered 238 destitute persons at various stations. 90 per cent of the Argyll force also qualified to render first aid to the injured.

An admirable state of efficiency is preserved by the capable officer Inspector MacCallum of Oban in his wide territory. Apart from Police Court proceedings innumerable claims upon time and attention are quietly attended to thus giving as far as possible practical effect to the call for 'Police Prevention of Crime'.[3]

What the report does not mention is that over the winter of 1926–27, there had been a noticeable increase in the instances of drunkenness that had been observed in the Ross of Mull. It was also evident that it was not due to ordinary commercial alcohol but to something more potent. Police enquiries led them to three brothers, Donald and Dugald MacKechnie, who lived at Brae, Bunessan, and Alexander MacKechnie, residing at Lee. All of them were labourers and, when brought before the Sheriff Court at Oban, would plead guilty to a charge of having failed to report the finding of a drum containing 40 gallons of a spirit with a powerful alcohol content which had been washed up on the shore near Ardlanish Point, in the Ross of Mull. They would have known they should have handed it over to the Receiver of Wreck for the district, but they drew off the spirit and hid the drum by burying it in a field on their small holding. The brothers were each fined £5 or 15 days' imprisonment. Procurator Fiscal Mackinnon added that during the winter, a large number of such drums had been coming ashore on the West Coast, and this was not the only instance in the South of Mull of the improper possession of spirits.

This incident was but a prequel compared to when the cargo ship SS *Politician* foundered on the sandbanks off Rosinish Point on the north coast of the Isle of Eriskay in the Outer Hebrides in 1941 with one of its holds full of Scotch whisky. An estimated 24,000 bottles of whisky 'salvaged' from the wreck by the islanders were never seen again. The

---

3. *Oban Times*, 18 February 1928

story inspired Compton Mackenzie to write his wonderful novel *Whiskey Galore* (1947) which was turned into the Ealing film of the same name in 1949. Slange Var!

Important changes had taken place in the Argyll County Police Force in 1927. The Chief Constable Major Allen was appointed HM Inspector of Constabulary for Scotland and Mr Donald Angus Ross from the Edinburgh force was appointed the new Chief Constable. Ross was most certainly a safe pair of hands for the role. Both Ross's father and brother were also serving Chief Constables and Donald would be in post as Chief Constable of Argyllshire for the next thirty years until his retirement in 1961.

When the rest of the highlands on the mainland experienced strife from disgruntled agricultural labourers in 1929, the islands still remained quiet. They were happy as they were and the rest could 'get on with it', and the police were more concerned with an outbreak of sheep scab on the Long Island, in Argyll and Inverness county and the resultant supervision of the dipping of over a million head of sheep in their area.

The police report for 1929 was a thorough one:

With every new crime the police are educated up to counter it and for this more foresight and greater insight are required. The heads of a police force have to be therefore men of exceptional ability. They have to consider their many masters – public opinion, for one thing: the coming of a changing form of criminality, the adoption of numberless Acts of Parliament, some good, some bad and some stupid. There are by-laws to be considered – the Urban and County rules, which work out differently. The quick decisions, the patient investigations, the numerous agricultural notices regarding sheep dipping, the movement of cattle, motoring offences and a host of other matters, which, summed up altogether make the position of Chief Constable so sinecure.

The administrative scheme of our two western counties is based upon admirable lines. The peculiar geographical difficulties of Argyll and Inverness, intersected by numerous waterways, necessitates a considerable extent of delegation of authority to divisional officers, so as to secure the prompt action requisite in official police work.

Each police division of Argyll, of which there are six, is under the charge of an experienced officer, Inspector or sergeant, who is capable of making responsible decisions and actions in cases of emergency, without reference to headquarters. How otherwise could this, the most essential of all police services, be carried on.

The Chief Constable has the responsibility of placing reliable officers, and we have never heard of a failure to undertake that routine and its details which should be impossible for one man to control, and be at a distance.

Chief Constable Ross and Major MacLean are to be congratulated upon their direction of the services which the police render in Argyll and Inverness. It is only by having reliable and experienced men stationed at the different sections of these widespread counties that the work can be successfully overtaken.

It must be a matter of anxiety and it says much of their intuition to select the best men, with the right of seniority duly considered. The efficiency of the two county constabularies is admirable and beyond question.

It is to the police to which the peaceable citizen looks for protection and the remarkably small number of crimes and offences is proof of the thoroughness of the organisation. The medical attitude towards crime is to cure it, but the disease is not discovered until it has broken out. The dog is not considered vicious until it has had its first bite. Similarly, the criminal might have done a deal of harm before the medical treatment come into operation. The police are the essential protectors of the public.

It is after realisation of the enormous and scattered areas of the counties of Argyll and Inverness, the diverse interests of a people on a far-off island, the inferior roads and backward public transport, with those of a population crowded into a town, that the full value of the service is apparent.

Taking the statistics of crimes and offences for Inverness-shire during 1929 we find only 378 convictions recorded, and in fourth of these the accused were under the influence of drink when the offence was committed. The remainder of convictions was in Fort William, where the number was 158 and half were committed when the offenders were under the influence of drink. Now that the hydro-electric works are completed, this number will diminish.

The statistics for Argyll are only entitled 'Police Report' which accords more with the practically crimeless condition of the county. There was only one individual remitted to the High Court and one tried by Sheriff and jury. Thirty was the total number of prisoners sent to Glasgow and Greenock Jails to serve a longer sentence than suitable for the local lock-ups.

It may be said therefore that the state of conduct in the two western counties is extremely satisfactory. And this satisfactory state is due to the efficient and loyal manner to which every officer in the service plays his part. Without making any distinction we would take this opportunity of congratulating our local chief, Inspector MacCullum, and his officers for the very able and satisfactory way in which they perform their duties and maintain good order in these parts.

In the 1920s, the officers of Scottish police forces were well respected, but their failure to adopt up-to-date policing methods, equipment and forensics left the forces at a disadvantage and were badly in need of reform. The changes across the police forces of Scotland would only happen gradually over time. Policing in Scotland would only begin to embrace the scientific advances in forensics in the following decade with no small thanks to the reforms and innovations of the newly appointed Chief Constable of the City of Glasgow, Sir Percy Sillitoe. The first step forward was made in 1931 with the appointment of Detective Sergeant Bertie Hammond, an expert in fingerprinting, who established a new Fingerprint and Photographic Department.

In a 1935 joint investigation carried out by City of Glasgow Police and Dumfriesshire Constabulary, the new fingerprinting techniques would be used to identify two dismembered bodies found near Moffat as the wife and maid of Lancaster-based doctor Buck Ruxton. The case became a national sensation and Ruxton would be tried and executed for the murders. But that was all yet to come; the attitude from many senior officers down to those on the beat back in 1929 was very much 'if it ain't broke, don't fix it.'

Advances in criminal psychology and profiling have come a long way over the past one hundred years but when investigating cases of suspicious deaths and murder that appear to involve elements of the occult, these can still be dismissed out of hand and, in so doing, can literally throw away some of the most valuable clues to solving a case. Investigators able to distance themselves from their own personal beliefs and sub-conscious prejudices for and against a belief in psychic powers have a greater advantage if they can carefully consider what the victim believed, and most importantly of all, how deeply they believed it?

When reading this book, it pays to remember much of the technology we take for granted today simply did not exist and the attitudes and beliefs of the 1920s were often different to ours today. It was the Jazz Age, a time modern audiences will know from *Thoroughly Modern Millie, Jeeves and Wooster, Peaky Blinders*, the murder mystery novels by Agatha Christie and their many TV and film adaptations. But when viewed with the benefit of hindsight, the reality was that the 'modern world' of the 1920s was also an age of naivety.

The notion of communication with the spirit world really took off from the mid-nineteenth century and enjoyed a massive revival during the First World War and throughout the 1920s when many sought news of their family and loved ones who had died or had been posted missing with no further explanation during the conflict. Seances were held in private houses and public venues where spirits apparently materialised through the auspices of apparently gifted mediums. The faces of the dear departed swathed in ectoplasm even appeared in photographs.

To our modern eyes, these 'spirit photographs' are crude trick images created in darkrooms, but to those seeing them at the time, they brought comfort, and there were plenty who would speak up in defence of their authenticity. The problem came when fraudulent mediums started to make quite a lot of money out of the bereaved. Magicians such as the famous American escapologist Harry Houdini and British stage magician William Marriot set about exposing the frauds, but there were still those who desperately wanted to cling to their beliefs and those who exposed the frauds ended up being treated rather like the kid who told the youngsters at school that there was no Santa Claus.

The man leading the vanguard in defence of communication with the spirit world and spirit photography was Sir Arthur Conan Doyle, the respected creator of the Sherlock Holmes stories. The bounds of his credibility, however, were pushed to the limit in the minds of the British public when he proclaimed the existence of fairies as a proven fact. The generation of the time had grown up with stories of fairies such as The Langs' Fairy Books published between 1889 and 1913, Arthur Rackham's wonderful illustrations and J. M. Barrie's *Peter Pan* (1904). Children dressed as fairies, pixies and sprites became staples of street parades, flower festivals and pageants through to the 1920s, but could Doyle have proof they really existed?

He did so based on photographs taken by two young girls, cousins Elsie Wright (16) and Frances Griffiths (9) at the beck in the village of Cottingley near Bradford, West Yorkshire in July 1917. Doyle published his conclusions in an article titled 'Fairies Photographed' published in *The Strand Magazine*, Christmas Number, 1920. The discovery was heralded as 'an epoch-making event' and Doyle would go on to publish further revelations in future articles and his book *The Coming of the Fairies* (1922). Others would join Doyle in his belief too and books like *Fairies at Work and Play* (1925) and *The Kingdom of the Faerie* (1927) by Geoffrey Hodson, that expounded theories surrounding the reality of fairies, would follow. Doyle was such a respected man the girls did not dare confess they had created hoax photographs until decades after Conan Doyle died in 1930.

For 'Flappers' and 'the pretty young things' with the money to enjoy it, the 1920s were a round of fashions and socialising, places to be seen and hedonistic parties to be, where alcohol flowed, smoking was daring and there was recreational drug use. For some men and women this was not enough. They wanted greater and greater highs, to explore forbidden knowledge, the esoteric and the exotic, without consideration of the dangers they were opening themselves up to. Most were far more vulnerable than they realised and some would fall prey to those who would deviously use the skills they had acquired in psychology, the powers of suggestion, the art of the magician and showmanship to their own extremely devious and dangerous ends.

'Armoured' by the arrogance of youth and a belief they knew what they were getting into, those enticed into the occult thought they could handle it and believed they were daring to draw back the curtain on forbidden mysteries and dark arts. Some would end up suffering terribly as a result. Some would pay for that adventure with their lives. One man stood out above all for such dark activities; his name was Aleister Crowley, who delighted in his biblical *nom de plume* of The Beast 666. In the 1920s and 1930s (before Hitler's evil behaviour became widely realised), Crowley was dubbed in the British press as 'The Wickedest Man in the World'.

The work of small, 'dark island' (called dark because of the absence of street lights) and Highlands policing changed little from the 1920s, the Scotland of *Whiskey Galore* in the 1940s up to the Hamish Macbeth murder mystery novels by M. C. Beaton (Marion Chesney) that first appeared in 1985 with *Death of a Gossip*. Adapted for television with Robert Carlyle in the lead role, the series first aired on BBC 1995–97 and the stories, set in and around the fictional Highland town of Lochdubh, show a gentle, rural Scotland with great characters and even have ghosts and a little magic thrown in for good measure.

The stories have a warm resonance with both those who are born and bred Scots and those who know and love the communities out in the wilds of Scotland. In reality, although there were very occasional fatal accidents or even bodies washed up on sea shores, suspicious deaths, let alone a murder, were and still are rare in these communities. Back in 1929, such incidents simply were not in the frame of reference for locals or police whose training or day-to-day duties really did not prime them for handling such occurrences as the discovery of the dead, body of a woman visitor staying on Iona being found on a lonely part of the island lying naked and frozen in a rough cross cut into the turf with a knife.

Over thirty years of researching the darkest history of Britain, I have been lucky enough to travel far and wide across our wonderful country. I have visited some amazing places, had privileged access to public and private archives and have met some fascinating people along the way. These include witches, wizards, and warlocks. Anyone who says that witches and witchcraft no longer exist in Britain is very much mistaken and they might be surprised to learn a coven or practicing witch can probably be found not far from them. I have also seen the vile evidence left behind by those who practice black magic rituals.

I have always attempted to carry out my research with empathy and objectivity, but I have occasionally come across stories and have visited locations that have truly made me shudder. A particular memory that comes to mind was when I was working with a group of American paranormal researchers in the Highlands of Scotland a few years ago. We visited the Boleskine Burial Ground, which nestles between the banks of Loch Ness and Boleskine House, where Aleister Crowley carried out some of his demonic rituals when he owned the property between 1899 and 1913.

At the time, I was aware of Crowley but had not immersed myself in the research and writing of this book. We had enjoyed uncommonly good sunny weather most of the week, but on this particular day, it was typically cold and wet in the Highlands. I really was not open to feeling anything much. It was such a miserable day as we left our warm coach to plod around the cemetery, but I felt *something* while I was there. Something I cannot easily describe other than a feeling that we were in the presence of something truly dark, and believe me, I have been in some places with some very dark history before, but they were nothing quite like this. Others felt it strongly too. There is much talk of Crowley never fully returning the demons he raised to where they came from … who knows? I am in no hurry to go back.

This book tells the story of Marie Fornario, a young woman known to some as Norah, the middle name she often used. To a select group of friends, she was known as Mac, for reasons that will be revealed over the following pages. Marie had a deep belief in the paranormal and she tried to do good with the mystical powers she believed she had. She died in mysterious circumstances on the remote Scottish island of Iona in November 1929. At the most prosaic level, I personally believe the cause of her death should have been investigated more thoroughly. I lay the facts surrounding her death as they are known before you in this book, along with the story of her life, many of the fascinating people she knew, 'the occult college' she attended and the secret mystical societies she was a member of. Please keep an open mind. Along the way, we will encounter stories of vampires, demons, witches, curses and the 'Wickedest Man in the World'.

Neil R. Storey
2025

Chapter 1

Cairo

Our story, which ends on a cold, dark night on the remote and windswept Hebridean island of Iona in 1929, about 46 miles off mainland Scotland, began four thousand miles away under blazing sun on the eastern shore of the river Nile, beneath the foothills of the Eastern Desert, amid the rocky promontories of the Muqaṭṭam Hills and the Al-Jabal al-Aḥmarin, in Cairo, Egypt in 1896.

Cairo had been a city for over a thousand years; to its northeast was the site of Heliopolis, where Plato once studied and discoursed on the immortality of the soul. On its southwestern edge are the Pyramids of Giza and to its east stands its City of the Dead (the district of Al-Qarāfah) with its extensive cemeteries, tombs, mausoleums and towering monuments of Mamluk design.

Within the semi-walled medieval city can be found architectural monuments from the times of the Romans, the Arabs and the Ottomans. Since the Anglo-Egyptian War in 1882, Egypt had been under British occupation and the bazaar and streets bustled with foreign traders and travellers like never before. In his book, *From Cairo to the Soudan Frontier* (1896), journalist and man of letters Henry Duff Traill observed and evocatively recorded this view from his Cairo hotel terrace while it was 'bathed in the morning glory of that peculiarly liquid sunshine which is almost a speciality of Egypt':

The colour and movement and perpetual play of light and shade on an ever-shifting mass of hues, that kaleidoscope of humanity which the ordinary every-day traffic of the Egyptian capital keeps twirling before the eyes … You step aside from one of the main thoroughfares, crowded with Western vehicles of every description, from the drag to a pony trap, and in an instant you are at once in a maze of alleys, where no draught animal of any kind has ever set foot since the houses were built on either side, and through which you may thread your way, surrounded by the same moving masses of colour for as many hours as you please without emerging again into Western civilisation.[1]

In 1896, the archaeology of Cairo and its surroundings were quite different to those which we know today. The Great Sphinx of Giza had only been partially excavated. Howard Carter had been in Egypt for just five years, the Valley of the Kings was little more than a hilly area of barren sand around a wadi on the west bank of the Nile and it would be over two more decades before Carter would discover the tomb of Tutankhamun and the fabulous treasures within it.

In the late nineteenth century, Cairo's skyline was unspoilt by modern high-rise buildings; only the domes of mosques and their minarets climbed skyward from which the muezzin's plaintive call to prayer would issue forth across the city five times a day. It was undoubtedly one of the most magnificent city skylines and a true wonder of the world to behold as the golden sun set behind the pyramids.

It was here, to Cairo, that Sherlock Holmes creator Arthur Conan Doyle travelled with his wife Louisa in late 1895 for an extended stay through winter into the spring of 1896. While Doyle was in Egypt, he travelled and witnessed conflict between British forces and dervishes and became a war correspondent for *The Westminster Gazette*.

He would also find the inspiration for his book *The Tragedy of the Korosko*, which was serialised in *The Strand Magazine* between May and December 1897 and published in book form in 1898. The story is a dramatic tale of a group of European tourists who were taking a trip along the Nile in a boat named the *Korosko* when they were set upon and abducted by a group of marauding dervishes and their subsequent escape to freedom.

---

1. Traill, Henry Duff, *From Cairo to the Soudan Frontier* (Lane, 1896)

What is far less well known is that Doyle had travelled to Egypt with his wife because she had been diagnosed with consumption two years previously.

The disease, commonly known as consumption (tuberculosis or 'TB'), was well known in Victorian Britain. It is a bacterial infection of the lungs that causes those suffering from it to have difficulty breathing, a persistent wet cough and fever that becomes progressively worse. In the latter stages, spots of blood would be coughed up among mucus, the patient would become languid and emaciated, fever would take over them and they would die. Those suffering from it would be seen to steadily 'waste away'. Because it was seen to be 'consuming' those afflicted by it, it was given the *nom de plume* 'consumption'.

The disease was spread through the wet cough and spitting of those suffering from it. It was particularly rife in the industrial towns and cities of Britain, where many people lived and worked in close proximity and affected both rich and poor alike. In the 1890s, consumption was still considered an 'incurable' disease. The life expectancy of someone suffering from tuberculosis in the 1890s was between three to five years. The symptoms and inevitable fatal progress of the disease could only be alleviated and its fatal progress delayed if sufferers had sufficient personal wealth or their families had enough money to be able to pay for extended periods in countries with warmer climates than that of Britain.

A certain Mrs Norah Fornario was in Cairo at the same time as the Doyles. Sadly, like Mrs Louisa Doyle, she also suffered from consumption. At that time, the well-to-do British citizens who could afford an extended stay in Cairo stood a good chance of staying at the same hotels as other British visitors. Mrs Fornario was also heavily pregnant. Her husband was, like Doyle, a medical doctor. Sadly, there is no evidence that they actually met but the Fornario's daughter, who would be born while they were in Cairo, would grow up to share many of the same esoteric interests as Doyle.

Mrs Fornario was born Norah Edith Ling in Manchester in 1865, the daughter of wealthy wholesale and retail tea merchant Thomas Pratt Ling and his wife Emily Ada Ling (née Turner). They went on to have two more children, both boys. George Duncan Ling was born at 15 Darlington Street, Cheatham Hill, Manchester, on 25 May 1866 and would become a director of the family tea and grocery business. His brother, Bertram Ling, born in Manchester on 28 August 1874, went on to become a director of his own wine and spirits business. Fortunately, both boys appear to have had good health, whereas, sadly, Norah did not.

The Lings, who were also evangelical Christians,[2] had sheltered their daughter's upbringing and were very keen that she should marry only the most appropriate suitor. The problem was by the late 1880s, she was in her late 20s and over the age most women of her class were expected to marry … then she was diagnosed with consumption.

It is highly likely that the Lings blamed themselves, at least in part, for their daughter contracting tuberculosis because their business caused them to live, work and raise their children in the densely populated cities of London and Manchester, where sanitation was poor and consumption was rife. Mr and Mrs Ling only wanted the best for Norah and they paid for her to spend much of her time in Italy and Egypt with a medical doctor of good standing to attend her. It must have come as quite some surprise to the Lings when, during Norah's stay in Italy, she became engaged to the Italian doctor who attended her – Dr Guiseppe Nicholo Raymondo Fornario MD of the Hospital Gesù e Maria, Naples. Dr Fornario must have been aware she not only had money, but the consumption she was suffering from meant she did not have long to live. Norah's parent's reaction is not recorded but some indication of their displeasure at the union would be seen in the provisions laid out in the codicils of the Will of Thomas Pratt Ling.

Dr Giuseppe Fornario was married to Miss Norah Ling by the Reverend Simon Mortlock Ranson at St Alban's Church, Streatham, on 7 September 1893. Norah became pregnant in 1895. It is not clear if she had planned to give birth while in Cairo or if her baby had arrived early. Egypt has only two seasons, four months of winter and eight months of summer, and May is just before the three hottest months of the year in Cairo when the days are a minimum of 70°F (21 °C) and can soar over 100°F. Norah's baby, who they named Marie Edith Emily Norah Fornario, was born on 7 May 1896. Norah returned to England with her baby in 1897. By that time, her consumption was in its advanced stages and was taking its toll on her. Norah died the following year, 1898, while at Christchurch, Hampshire, aged just 33.

---

2. HO 144-1765-431695 Nationality and Naturalisation papers: Statement by Fornario, Marie Norah Emily Edith

Chapter 2

The Cloistered Girl

I have seen happy dreams rise up and pass,
Silent and swift as shadows on the grass.
Fiona MacLeod

Little Marie Fornario was just one year old when her mother died and she was placed in the care of her grandparents (Norah's Mother and father), Thomas and Emily Ling. She grew up with them at their lovely home of Leigham Holme, Leigham Court Road, Streatham Hill. It was the sort of mid-Victorian new-build home that was the epitome of a prosperous Victorian businessman. It had a gated driveway off a leafy, quiet road. The property was detached and set in its own grounds and was maintained by a small retained staff, listed in the 1901 census as Jane Cole (29) governess, Matilda Slapp (24) parlour maid, Florence Hudson (30) cook, and Kate Hudson (23) housemaid. They also had a coachman, Robert Mason (58), who lived at The Stables with his wife Hannah (54).

The Lings would move a few years later to another lovely residence known as 'Bracondale' in Dorking, Surrey. Tragically, young Marie's life was turned upside down yet again when her grandmother, Emily Ling, died at home on 18 February 1908, aged 66. Exactly a year and a day later, Marie's grandfather, Thomas Pratt Ling, also died at home from a heart attack on 19 February 1909, aged 73. Now aged just 12 years old, Marie had lost her mother and both grandparents. Her absent father took no interest in her nor her upbringing.[1] She was, however, left a small fortune of £12,000 (£1,779,103.18 in today's money) by her grandfather, but the conditions laid down for her to receive the money were so uniquely

---

1. HO 144-1765-431695 Nationality and Naturalisation papers: Statement by Fornario, Marie Norah Emily Edith

specific it was printed as a newsworthy article in numerous provincial papers after the Will was proved:

> Provided that she shall remain under the guardianship of his son George Duncan Ling or other person approved by his trustees and shall not forsake the English Protestant Faith, or marry person not of that Faith, or marry a first cousin on either her father's or her mother's side, under penalty of losing one-half of her interest in this sum. [2]

The Will also stipulated that the income should be paid to her in the United Kingdom, 'unless for a cause to be certified by medical certificate, or other cause to be approved by his trustees'.[3]

A note on Marie's nationalisation papers written by her solicitor added:

> These elaborate provisions were made for the purpose of preventing the child becoming under the influence of her father, who is a Roman Catholic, but when the father found that he could not obtain any control over the funds to which his daughter was entitled he never interfered with her education or upbringing and took no interest whatever in her since the death of her grandfather.[4]

Marie's Guardians and Trustees of the Will were now her uncle and aunt, George Duncan Ling and his wife, Florence Hannah Ling. The couple did not have any children of their own. Marie would live with them at a fine house named 'Trenton' in Reigate, Surrey, from June 1909 until 1915. She would then move with them to Blanford Cottage, Reigate and would reside with them there from 1915 to February 1920. On the 1911 census, when Marie was aged sixteen, she was recorded as a boarder at The Ladies College, Grassington Road, Eastbourne. She would also be recorded over the years as a boarder at Malvern House Girls School, Reading; at Westcliff Girls Boarding School, Weston-super-Mare and finally attended Eastbourne School of Cookery at 11 Silverdale Road, Eastbourne.

---

2. *Bayswater Chronicle*, 17 April 1909
3. *Bayswater Chronicle*, 17 April 1909
4. TNA file: HO 144-1765-431695

Why Marie attended several different schools is unclear; it was not as if her guardians were moving around the country or the fees were beyond their pocket nor the funds provided from her grandfather's Will. Her handwriting is neat and her surviving articles are articulate and show her as a woman of intelligence and culture. So one can only imagine the reasons why Marie did not thrive or remain at the schools chosen for her. What few clues we have come from Iona Cammell (née McDonald) (1903–1981), who was acquainted with Marie, and had spoken to those who had come to know her shortly before her untimely death for an article about her under the title of *The Sorceress of the Isles* in the first edition of *The Atlantis Quarterly* in 1932.[5] Iona also shared her recollections of Marie with Alasdair Alpin MacGregor:

She was of a frank and friendly disposition … and readily made friends … however she had been some time in their midst before telling them anything very personal about herself. She did eventually say that her Italian father was a professor of something or other at some Italian university, and that her mother, a London lady of means, had died while she was still a child. With the English uncle and aunt in London, who had brought her up, she had never been happy. They were apt to be impatient with her: they could not understand her temperament. Her father she had not seen for many a year. The passage of time seemed to have intensified her bitterness towards him, apparently for his having married an unsuitable Englishwoman, her mother. The children of such marriages, she held, were often doomed to misfortune.[6]

What little else is recorded of Marie's young life is she already showed promise as a writer in 1917 when aged 21. *Memories of the Deep. Four sea idylls, written by M Fornario*, as performed by the soprano Gertrude Bracey, was published as sheet music. During the spring and summer of that same year, the First World War was still grinding on and Marie became a volunteer worker at an Auxiliary War Hospital for wounded

5. Iona's husband, Richard Charles Cammell (1903–1981), was a biographer of Aleister Crowley and was, with Lewis Spence, co-editor of *The Atlantis Quarterly*
6. MacGregor, Alasdair Alpin, *The Ghost Book* (Hale 1955)

soldiers who had been evacuated to Britain from the battlefields of the Western Front. The hospital where she served had been established in a fine Victorian villa known as 'Kempston' on the corner of Granville and Blackwater Roads in Eastbourne. It was one of around 3,000 Auxiliary War Hospitals established in public buildings and large private houses around the country during the war.

Known locally as Kempston Red Cross Hospital, it had been opened in March 1915 by Mrs Davies-Gilbert and Miss Helena Catherine Sulman, Commandant of Red Cross Voluntary Aid Detachment (VAD) Sussex 118. It consisted of six large wards with a total of 38 beds over three floors. The wounded suffering the most serious cases were on the ground floor and first floor, the less serious on the top floor. Patients were attended by local doctors, four trained nurses, and forty local women who served as part-time VAD nurses who worked on rotas to provide 24-hour care. There were also certified uniformed volunteers helping to maintain the likes of stores, laundry and kitchens.

Marie was not attached to any unit but had been trained, passed her exams and held British Red Cross Society certificates in First Aid and Home Nursing. Her duties appear to have been limited to scullery work in the evenings, probably consisting of washing up and assisting the kitchen staff. When not engaged in their assigned duties, the hospital staff were encouraged to interact with the patients, to visit them and have a chat, read to them or help them write letters home. Marie would have been in the hospital when casualties were returned from The Battle of Arras. She would have been around the same age as many of the young men in those hospital beds. One can only imagine the effects of war she saw on those men, their shattered bodies, lost limbs, lost sight, infected wounds, broken and damaged minds and the impressions it left upon Marie. Vera Brittain was a volunteer nurse during the First World War and powerfully wrote of the legacy of thoughts caring for the wounded left her with in *Testament of Youth* (1933):

Already this was a different world from the one that I had known during four life-long years, a world in which people would be light-hearted and forgetful, in which themselves and their careers and their amusements would blot out political ideals and great national issues. And in that brightly lit, alien world I should have no part. All those with whom I had really been intimate were gone; not one remained to share with me the heights and the depths of my memories. As the years went by and youth departed and remembrance great dim, a deeper and ever deeper darkness would cover the young men who were once my contemporaries.

Chapter 3

Crossing the Rubicon

Ālea iacta est – The die has been cast

Julius Caesar

In 1920, Marie Fornario was ready to spread her wings. She had control of her money and was ready to embark on new adventures, both in this world and particularly the esoteric and spiritual worlds. It has not proved possible to find which friendship provided the introductions for Marie to cross the Rubicon and join her first secret society or exactly when this took place. What is known is Violet Mary Firth, who will be best known as the author and occultist Dion Fortune and one of the foremost pioneers of modern magic, would describe knowing Marie 'intimately and at one time we did a great deal of work together...' in her book *Psychic Self-Defence: A Study in Occult Pathology and Criminality* (1930).

Sadly, Violet did not mention how and when she and Marie had met but in her preface to *Psychic Self-Defence*, she writes that when she was in her twenties she was in the employ of a woman who had spent many years in India and had acquired considerable knowledge of 'mind-power'.[1] Violet did not name the woman but she can be identified as Dr Lilias Hamilton, the Warden of Studley Horticultural & Agricultural College for Women in Warwickshire. According to Firth, Hamilton did not use her mind powers to good ends, instead, she used them to control and influence those working under her to the degree that a number of them had suffered mental breakdowns.

Among those who fell under Hamilton's influence was a young girl Violet described as 'an orphan with considerable means'.[2] Hamilton made sure the girl remained close by her side at all times; she won over her confidence, got into her mind and managed to persuade the girl to put

---

1. Fortune, Dion *Psychic Self-Defence: A Study in Occult Pathology and Criminality* (Rider, 1930)
2. Fortune, Dion *Psychic Self-Defence: A Study in Occult Pathology and Criminality* (Rider, 1930)

her entire financial reserves into her schemes. Fortunately, the girl had trustees to oversee her money and Violet describes how they 'descended in wrath, forced my employer to disgorge, and took the girl away with them then and there, leaving all her belongings behind, to be packed up and sent on to her afterwards'. In the end, Violet suffered a breakdown, which she was convinced had been caused by the mind control techniques that Hamilton used on her.

At a public lecture Violet presented on her occult experiences in 1925, she recalled these events, as the report of the talk recounted in the newspaper:

This woman [*Hamilton*]had a very uncanny power over her, and at times, when under the woman's influence, she could actually feel her soul being drawn out of her body. At such times she experienced a narrowing of her field of vision, a sense of imminent darkness, and she struggled to get free. An inner voice, in definite articulation told her what to do in order to break loose from this undesirable 'spell'. She gained her freedom, but it took her three years to recover from the effects.[3]

It is very tempting to suggest the young orphan girl Violet describes might have been Marie Fornario; the chances are slim but this experience left a vivid impression on Violet. It would undoubtedly have come to mind when Violet and Marie got to know each other and could have been one of those relationship strands that led to deeper and stronger bonds of friendship between such spiritual souls.

The earliest document that connects Violet Firth and Marie Fornario is a list of ritual officers for the year 1919–1920 at a Lodge of Co-Freemasonry (for men and women) that held its lodge meetings at the home of a certain Theodore William Carte Moriarty (more of whom later) at 26 Sinclair Road, Hammersmith, W14. This fine Victorian three-storey house has now been divided into flats. The largest of the flats today has advertised it as being spread over 710 square feet, so in Moriarty's day, when he had the run of the entire house, he would have

---

3. *Bayswater Chronicle*, 28 March 1925

had the space for a lodge and to live there. It would, of course, mean that rather than staging meetings amid the awe of a lofty hall, the gatherings would have been far more intimate.

Such a set-up was far from unusual and many of the witch covens and magical secret societies that exist in London today meet and enact their rituals under similar conditions in private homes, in hired rooms above shops and offices and even in cellars under high street business premises. The Isis Urania Temple of the Second Order of The Golden Dawn was situated on the first floor of 63 Blythe Road, Olympia, West Kensington W14, on the border with Hammersmith. Infamously, in an incident that rapidly became steeped in legend, it was the scene of a 'psychic battle' between W B Yeats and Aleister Crowley on 19 April 1900. Crowley stormed in dressed in Highland garb, wearing a black mask of Osiris, a plaid thrown over his head and shoulders, an enormous gold or gilt cross on his breast, and a dagger at this side and attempted to seize leadership of the group.

Some accounts tell of how Yeats translated his powerful thoughts into the medium of his physical leg and foot and booted Crowley back down the stairs. In other, more prosaic accounts, Crowley was stopped by the landlord. It was pointed out to Crowley that there was no way he could assume power because the lease was not in his name and he was compelled to leave by members and a policeman who had been summoned to the scene.

Just a three-minute walk away from Blythe Road was 26 Sinclair Road, Hammersmith, the home of Theodore William Carte Moriarty and it was there he established The Hammersmith Lodge Co-Masonic Group twenty years later. It was not officially recognised by the Grand Lodge and, ultimately, it could not be regulated or penalised by them either if it did not blacken the name of Freemasonry. If he led it well and charismatically, the group would flourish, Moriarty could pick and choose his members as he pleased and all would proceed in peace and harmony.

According to a surviving published list of the officers of the Lodge, Violet Firth was listed as Junior Warden and Marie Fornario as Outer Guard. Marie was given a very responsible position for one so new to Freemasonry. She must have been quite a formidable character when she needed to be. The Outer Guard (also known as the Tyler) had the duty of guarding the door of the lodge armed with a sword. It was the duty of the Outer Guard to ensure that only those qualified to do so enter the lodge, their worthiness to proceed being proved by an exchange of words, signs and tokens. It would also fall to the Outer Guard to make sure candidates were properly prepared for initiation. The position is usually occupied by one of the older, stalwart members of the lodge.

Moriarty was listed as Master or Adeptus and appears to have been the only male officer. He seems to have preferred the latter title in his correspondence. It is an unusual one, more regularly used in the Societas Rosicruciana in Anglia, a separate society within Freemasonry made up of Christian Master Masons that focuses on Rosicrucian philosophy. Most male-only Masonic Lodges do not recognise Co-Freemasonry, holding it to be 'irregular'. The Hammersmith Lodge, however, had no problem recruiting new candidates and carried out thirteen initiations and an affiliation during the year.

Moriarty was a remarkable character. Born at 5 Upper Gloucester Street, North City, Dublin, Ireland on 27 July 1873, his birth certificate states his name as Theodore William Moriarty; his middle name 'Carte' does not appear on it. He was the youngest son of Crimean war veteran Captain William Moriarty, one of a line of Royal Navy officers. His great-grandfather was Vice Admiral Sylverius Moriarty (1735–1809), Vice Admiral of the White Squadron. Theodore Moriarty did gain a cadetship in the Royal Navy in 1886[4] but, clearly, he was not as suited to naval life as his ancestors had been and joined the Army. His birth certificate appears among the UK Officer's Birth Certificates and papers (formerly Public Record Office[5]) now lodged in the National Archives and in the mid-1890s, he was described in the press as 'late Dublin Fusiliers'. [6]

In the 1890s, Moriarty was diagnosed with tuberculosis. This would certainly have brought his military career to an end and he was advised to emigrate to South Africa for its climate if he was going to have any hope of recovering from the disease. Moriarty did go to South Africa, enjoyed a remarkable recovery and was fortunate to find work surveying roads, so he got plenty of fresh air. He then found employment as a customs officer.

---

4. *Romsey Register and General News Gazette,* 16 December 1886
5. PRO WO/42/70 (II)
6. *Freeman's Journal,* 5 August 1896

While in South Africa, Moriarty developed a great interest in African folklore and tribal customs. He also married Georgina Kate Croly on 7 September 1896 at Port Elizabeth (now Gqeberha) in Eastern Cape Province. Georgina was the fourth daughter of Henry Gray Croly, FRCS, County Dublin, Surgeon of Dublin Hospital and past President of the College of Surgeons, who lived at number 7 in the exclusive Merrion Square, Dublin, where both the families of Yeats and Wilde had lived. Both having sons who would go on to become such literary icons. Georgina stated no occupation or calling for herself on the marriage certificate but Moriarty describes himself simply as a 'Capitalist'.

The couple would be blessed with five children. Sadly, a son was stillborn in 1900 and a daughter Kathleen, born in 1901, did not live long but three other children lived to maturity: Sylvia Norah Ethel, born in 1898, Lewis William (who was also known as William Lewis), born in 1906, and Denis Redmond born shortly after their return to England in 1908.

Moriarty had been initiated as a Freemason while in South Africa and he carried on Freemasonry when he made his home in England. In documents, he signed himself as being of the 18th degree, reflecting yet again his pride in his membership of the Rosicrucian society within Freemasonry. He would co-author *Notes on Masonic Etiquette and Jurisprudence* with Thomas N. Cranstoun-Day, first published in 1908 and *The Freemason's Vade Mecum* in 1909.

After their arrival in England, the Moriartys initially lived at Paignton, Devon, then moved to Chiswick, Middlesex. On the 1911 census, Moriarty, his wife and three children and their live-in governess, Marguerita Willikins, are recorded as residing at Flat 6, 28 Colville Square, Notting Hill, West London. Moriarty states his profession as shipping clerk. They next moved a short distance away to 9 Hereford Mansions, Hereford Road, Bayswater.

In 1913, Moriarty began an affair with Irish-born Miss Sophie Louise D'Elsa during a visit to Spain. He then began visiting her at her flat at Alexandra Mansions in Maida Vale and then left the family home in August 1914 and began cohabiting with Miss D'Elsa. Mrs Moriarty filed for divorce in 1914, citing adultery as the reason. The Decree Nici was granted on 16 April 1915 and Moriarty was ordered to pay her legal costs and £2 a week alimony.

At the time of the divorce, Georgina had moved away with the children to Weston-super-Mare and Moriarty stated he was now a Refreshment House Proprietor living with Miss D'Elsa at 275 High Holborn, London, WC.[7] This relationship ended during the First World War. Miss D'Elsa would subsequently emigrate to America, marry a medical student named William James Guy and settle in Monrovia, Los Angeles, California. She would die there aged 39 in May 1922, the month after she gave birth to her daughter Raydia.

After the end of the affair that ended his marriage, Moriarty went to live alone at Flat 9, Hereford Mansions, South Paddington. He also reinvented himself. The title of 'Dr' begins to appear with his name and he would claim he studied at Dublin and at Heidelberg universities, but unless he did so under another name, no evidence to support this has emerged to date, even after several researchers have attempted to find it over the years. Despite being known as 'Dr' Moriarty, there is nothing to support that qualification, be it medical or in any other sphere of recognised academia for that matter.

A story attached to Theodore Moriarty is that he was a friend of Arthur Conan Doyle who, so the story goes, is said to have expressed his interest in joining Freemasonry and other secret esoteric societies to which Moriarty belonged but Moriarty declined to sponsor his candidacy. Doyle and he suffered a spat as a result and Doyle named his greatest character's brilliant but evil nemesis Moriarty to spite him.

It is a struggle to find any truth in the story (and that is being kind). Doyle was first initiated into Freemasonry at Phoenix Lodge No. 257 in Southsea, Portsmouth in 1887 when he was aged 27. At that time, Moriarty would have been 14 years old and too young to be initiated into Freemasonry. Doyle's Professor Moriarty made his first appearance in the short story *The Adventure of the Final Problem* published in *The Strand Magazine* in December 1893. It is doubtful Doyle and Moriarty had met at that time and Moriarty was not initiated into Freemasonry until after he emigrated to South Africa in 1896. It is a safe bet, however, that Moriarty would have enjoyed the notoriety of his surname being

---

7. Ancestry.co.uk England & Wales, Civil Divorce Records, 1858–1918, 05948 Moriarty

the inspiration for 'the Napoleon of Crime'. In fact, he may well have created the story in the first place.

Violet Firth first met Moriarty when she was aged 26 and was working as a lay therapist at the Medico-Psychological Clinic at 30 Brunswick Square, Bloomsbury, in 1916. The clinic was seen as ground-breaking in its day. Founded in 1913 by Dr Jessie Murray and Julia Turner, the clinic provided therapy and training in psychoanalysis from qualified medical practitioners as well as those who had evident skills but no formal qualifications. When Moriarty was first brought into the clinic, it was because of his reputation as a teacher of a system that he dubbed 'Universal Theosophy' through which he apparently managed to pacify and even cure a number of patients that had defied treatment until he had become involved.

Violet Firth was so enraptured by Moriarty she was inspired to write her first short stories, which she claimed were fictionalised accounts of Moriarty's genuine cases retold under the guise of Dr Taverner, who ran a mysterious nursing home that dealt with patients suffering from unusual psycho-physical problems who were treated by Taverner using his unorthodox methods. Taverner recruited a medical superintendent for his nursing home and the position was filled by Dr Rhodes, who soon finds himself assisting Taverner in his adventures in a similar manner as Dr Watson did for Sherlock Holmes. Violet based Dr Rhodes on herself. Although her Dr Rhodes was male, they shared characteristics and both he and Violet were recovering from nervous breakdowns.

The Secrets of Dr Taverner was first published as a serial in *The Royal Magazine* in February-July 1922. It would also be Violet's first appearance in print under her pen name of Dion Fortune. She would later write candidly in the introduction to the book of the stories *The Secrets of Dr Taverner* published in 1926 'if there had been no Dr Taverner, there would have been no Dion Fortune'.

Gareth Knight would describe Moriarty as a man who was 'a Mason of considerable erudition' who was also blessed with 'remarkable occult abilities, and wide ranging freedom of thought'. Moriarty certainly had a charisma about him and he seemed to be able to attract loyal followers to his teachings, notably three sisters; Elsie Reeves, Ursula Allen-Williams and Gwen Stafford-Allen, all of them daughters of Francis Allen and his first wife Charlotte Dickson who died in 1912. Francis Allen then married Dorothy Combe, who had inherited Cockley Cley Hall in Norfolk. Mr Allen was a gentleman Egyptologist and sponsor of Howard Carter. The three Allen sisters were sponsors of Moriarty. Elsie and Ursula provided Moriarty with temporary premises on their properties for him to present his lectures but Gwen went further and employed both Moriarty and Violet Firth in a unique venture.

Chapter 4

The Occult College

Into this calm environment let the ominous thing put out its head, unobtrusively at first, and then more insistently, until it holds the stage.

M R James

In May 1919, Gwen Stafford-Allen used inherited money to purchase The Grange, Bishop's Stortford, Hertfordshire, the former residence of Sir John Barker, for her new business venture – The Science, Arts and Crafts Association Ltd to create 'an institution for the physical and mental improvement of both sexes during convalescence from illness'.[1]

In 1921, The Grange was advertising under the banner of the Science, Arts and Crafts Association, offering 'A Course of Domestic Economy including household management, cooking and dressmaking' commencing in the autumn term from 22 September 1921. Both boarders and day students were welcome but the courses offered a lot more than appeared in the adverts.[2] A later newspaper article published in the *Yorkshire Post* under the title 'An Educational Experiment' explained more of Gwen Stafford-Allen's vision:

Education, always in process evolution, has made rapid strides in the last twenty-five years but many thinkers believe that it has not yet reached its highest point of development and that in the future it will run on lines which, at present, we can only see faint indications.

The wholesale stuffing of children's minds with unco-ordinated and uncorrected facts is rapidly going out fashion and some interesting experiments, all striving for the same goal, though somewhat different means are now being made in England. The object of the Domestic Science College at the Grange, Bishop's Stortford, as Miss Allen,

---

1. *Suffolk Free Press*, 21 May 1919
2. *Herts and Essex Observer*, 13 August 1921

the director, explained to me recently, is "to open the mind's interests by giving the pupil an elementary bird's eye view of evolution, and furnish her with a mental concept which, later on, when she meets with emotional experiences which might otherwise knock her over, will provide point of view that will keep her steady.

"In other words, not to 'stuff' but to draw out that which she has in herself, and provide her with philosophy that will enable her to recognise the essentials in everything and realise that it is the thought behind the action that really matters".

Concurrently with the Domestic Science teaching there is a course of 39 specially prepared lectures, the subjects of which are arranged that they weave into each other, enabling the student to see how comparative religion depends on psychology, psychology on anthropology, and anthropology on the conditions under which man, as a species has evolved.

"Realisation of the Unity Life, the interdependence all its parts, and the one-ness of Man with the other kingdoms," Miss Allen continued "broadens the interests and gives a philosophic and metaphysical outlook upon, and interpretation of, emotion and events which cannot fail to be useful in later years.

Before such training can be attempted, the pupil must, of course, have the usual foundations of knowledge, mathematics, history and so on."

The attention of the teacher on these lines is not, however, confined to the mind. Physical exercises such 'jerks' or Dalcroze Eurythmics, the acting of plays of serious purpose, and even manual labour of the lighter kind – in a garden, for example – are actively encouraged, the underlying purpose being to make the emotional as well the physical body healthy and sound and enable the girls to co-ordinate their faculties and knowledge and acquire the power, of standing outside, as it were, viewing life from the abstract and thus acquiring not only understanding but also steady mental poise and complete emotional control.

Here, team work is of special value, and in this connection reference to Antioch College in America, may not be out of place. Every student there takes the full University course but while doing so has to earn it, work being temporarily found by the Principal which will not only develop the student's talents and abilities but also bring him into contact with and increase his knowledge of humanity.

"Obviously," Miss Allen concluded, "both in America and England the system is in the experimental stage but as time goes on I hope it will more and more widely applied general education. It is more successful in small classes than in large and would probably find its highest expression in mixed-educational schools."[3]

To those who came to work and study in the science department of this educational establishment, they were under no illusions that this was no ordinary seat of learning, indeed one of its lecturers, Violet Firth (Dion Fortune) would refer to it as The Occult College.[4] Although a bed would always be waiting for her when she was lecturing at The Grange, Violet would continue to work as a medical psychologist and lecturer from her home base in a bedsit she rented from Mrs Elizabeth Bailey at 120 Fellow Road in Hampstead. A residence where the other room was taken by Harold Dinsly Jennings White (26), a conscientious objector who had been imprisoned at Wormwood Scrubs for his beliefs during the First World War. On the 1921 census, he is shown as a part-time psychology student who also worked at 30 Brunswick Square.

Studious as ever, Marie Fornario took up residence as a boarder at The Grange on 27 February 1920.[5] Marie appears on the 1921 census aged 25 still as a boarder at The Grange and states her personal occupation as 'Student, Science Department: Science, Arts and Crafts Association'.

Marie embraced her new academic life with enthusiasm and presented her first known lecture, 'Myths of the Norse,' at the second meeting of the Spring Term of the Bishop's Stortford Students' Association held at the town's Technical Institute on the evening of Monday, 21 February 1921. She was in good company on a programme of monthly lectures that included Miss T. Kewley, BA, of Chantry Mount School, who lectured on 'The Social Importance of Heraldry in the Middle Ages', Mr E W

---

3. *Yorkshire Post and Leeds Intelligencer,* Monday 20 July 1925

4. Fortune, Dion, *Psychic Self-Defence: A Study in Occult Pathology and Criminality* (Rider, 1930)

5. TNA HO 144-1765-431695

Edmunds, BSc, on 'Radium' and Miss Fildes, BSc, of Hockerill Training College on 'Memory'.

Marie had a good audience and was given a warm vote of thanks by the group's president, Dr Young. Sadly, Marie does not appear to have written up her research into a published paper; at least no copy of it has been found to date, but fortunately, an account of her lecture was published in the *Herts and Essex Observer* on Saturday, 26 February 1921 and it is reproduced in full in Appendix 1

When Marie applied for and was granted British citizenship (then known as naturalisation) in 1922, she would again state her occupation as student and give The Grange as her home address.[6] Marie Fornario was no ordinary student on a course of specific duration. She was serving an apprenticeship in occult science.

The 1921 census also shows Gwen Stafford Allen (37), the owner of the Grange, as Chairman & Head of Science, Arts and Crafts Association and her niece, Elizabeth Alleyne Reeves (12), also shown as living with her. Gwen and Marie had two notable things in common in that they both had family roots in the county of Norfolk (Marie's maternal grandfather had been born in Norwich) and both Gwen and Marie had been born in ancient capitals of Egypt – Marie in Cairo and Gwen in Ramleh, Alexandria.

The staff at The Grange consisted of House Superintendent, Gwendolen Meta Williams (36), a Cook, Olive Winifred Grace Upfold (24), Caterer Amelia Mabel Campbell (39) and house servants, Doris Cole (17) and Julia Amy Fish (16).

Major Francis Robert Seymour RAMC (38), a Medical Officer in the Ministry of Health, Whitehall, London and his wife Ida Minnie Seymour (32), a Medical Practitioner of the Public Health Department, London County Council, and their twin daughters Rosamund and Ruth (2) along with their children's nurse Minnie Alice Johnson (26) were recorded as visitors with a home address in London.

Marie's fellow boarding students are recorded as Claudia Oakes (19) of Sloane Square, London (whose mother Amelia Oaks (51) of Paddington was also visiting at the time of the census) and Charlotte Evelyn Stafford

---

6. TNA HO 334-94

(43) of Nottingham. Both Oakes and Stafford are shown as students of Art and Science Departments, whereas Marie states she is solely a student of the Science Department.

The Art Department lecturer (and co-worker) was Natalie Olga Charlotte Cazalet (64), who had been Resident British-born in Petrograd, Russia. The Science Department was undoubtedly the domain of Theodore William Carte Moriarty (50), who described himself as Lecturer and co-worker, with Joan Helen Violet Williams (35) as co-worker and Honorary Secretary, Science Department.

Oddly, rather than stating his place of birth on the census as Dublin, Moriarty is recorded on the census as Resident British-born in Esquimalt, (a municipality at the southern tip of Vancouver Island), British Columbia, Canada. Perhaps he was trying to distance himself from the Irish Civil War that was raging at the time in his native country after the signing of the Anglo-Irish Treaty.

Or it may also be possible that he was trying to align himself more with Algernon Blackwood, one of the masters of the modern ghost story genre and a member of the Golden Dawn. Blackwood was British-born, at Shooter's Hill, but he had worked as a dairy farmer in Canada, operated a hotel and had been one of the founding members of the Toronto Theosophical Society in 1891. Marie Fornario was much enamoured with Blackwood and described his *Prisoner in Fairyland* (1913) as 'a perfect expression of spiritual truth'.[7]

It was during Moriarty's time at The Grange that several of his most dramatic and disturbing cases took place. In *The Secrets of Dr Taverner*, Violet changed the identity of The Grange at Bishop's Stortford to what she described as 'the mysterious nursing home' where Dr Taverner's patients came for treatment. She also relocated the establishment to the Hampshire barrens around Hindhead, where it stood amid a 'blighted landscape' and an 'unchristian spot'[8] where locals still observed and maintained faith in elements of pagan ritual more for luck or superstition rather than knowledge of its 'inner meaning'. The home itself was described by Dr Rhodes in the story as:

7. Tyler, Mac (Marie Farnario), *The Use of Imagination in Science, Art and Business*, *The Occult Review*, vol 48 No1 July 1928

8. Fortune, Dion, *The Secrets of Dr Taverner* (Noel Douglas, 1926)

in delightful contrast to the wild and barren country that surrounded it. The garden was a mass of colour, and the house, old and rambling and covered by creepers, as charming within as without; it reminded me of the East, it reminded me of the Renaissance, and yet it had no style save that of warm rich colouring and comfort.[9]

At the time Violet and Marie knew The Grange, it was set away from the main town of Bishop's Stortford. According to the sale advertisement for The Grange published in *Country Life*, the property was sold as 'Within an hour of town' (meaning London) and consisted of five fine reception rooms, a billiard room, fourteen bed and dressing rooms and three bathrooms. Its grounds were described as 'pretty' and were surrounded by well-timbered park-like lands of about thirteen acres. The house was also fitted out with electric light, 'excellent drainage and water' and stabling for six horses.[10]

Historic photographs of The Grange and Violet's description of the fictional Dr Taverner's nursing home chime well with each other but one can only wonder what Marie witnessed and to what degree was she involved in Moriarty's case work there. Violet was always mindful not to name those involved in the cases she personally witnessed, as she explained:

In my novel, 'The Secrets of Dr. Taverner', there were presented, under the guise of fiction, a number of cases illustrative of the hypotheses of occult science. Some of these stories were built up to show the operation of the invisible forces; others were drawn from actual cases; and some of these were written down rather than written up in order to render them readable by the general public.[11]

---

9. Fortune, Dion, *The Secrets of Dr Taverner* (Noel Douglas, 1926)
10. *Country Life*, 4 August 1917
11. Fortune, Dion, *Psychic Self-Defence: A Study in Occult Pathology and Criminality* (Rider, 1930)

Chapter 5

Vampires

In this enlightened age, when men believe not even what they see, the doubting of wise men would be his greatest strength.

Dracula, Bram Stoker

Today, it is recognised in psychiatric medicine that there are a number of mental disorders that can cause those suffering from them to manifest the behaviours of a vampire and even drink blood. In the 1920s, the understanding of these conditions and mental illness in general was far less advanced but anyone, then or now, confronted by the actions of a human being possessed with the utmost conviction that they are indeed a vampire and are acting accordingly must be terrifying. Or for those who believe in the darker paths of the paranormal … vampires *do* exist and they are not all bound by all the folkloric 'rules' laid out in literature, such as that found in Bram Stoker's classic novel *Dracula* (1897).

Cases of modern vampirism tend not to be carried out by the undead, who rise from their graves after dark to seek out their victims. Instead, those suffering from the mind disorder (or is it?), believe the entity takes spirit form, possesses the body of a living person and causes them to seek out blood, preferably human, but mammalian would suffice, and drink it. The ingested blood gives the spirit vampire its power. The living, in effect, become blood-sucking 'batteries' for the vampire. The human bitten by those possessed by the spirit of the vampire can also become subject to the contagion, be possessed by the entity and operate as another bloodsucker providing him, or her, with yet more power to draw upon.

In Violet Firth's fictionalised story 'Blood Lust', published under her pen name of Dion Fortune as the opening chapter of her Royal Magazine serial *The Secrets of Dr. Taverner* in 1922, Dr Taverner and his assistant Dr Rhodes are confronted by a case of vampirism. In her introduction to the book of the series published in 1926, Firth states that the story is 'literally true' and adds that far from being written up for the purposes of fiction, it had been 'toned down to make it fit for print'.[1] In the fictional story, she describes how a male patient, former army officer Captain Donald Craigie, sets out to sate his blood lust by attacking animals and people in secret and under the cover of darkness by swinging down the 'ropes of wisteria that clothed the wall' of Taverner's nursing home. Early twentieth-century photographs of The Grange in Bishop's Stortford show its frontage well covered in mature wisteria.

Firth revisits her account of the case without fictionalisation in *Psychic Self Defence* (1930) and reveals the incident had actually occurred while she was working with Moriarty at the Brunswick Square clinic. The case was first brought to their notice by the family of an afflicted young man who she quaintly describes as 'a youth in the late teens, one of the degenerate but intellectual and socially presentable types that not infrequently crop up in old families whose blood is too blue to be wholesome'.[2]

The young man had got into a habit of visiting and sitting with a cousin who had been invalided home from the battlefields of France, apparently with 'shell-shock'. The truth of the matter told by the parents of the younger man to Moriarty and Firth was that the 'shell-shocked' cousin had, in fact, been 'caught in the act of necrophilia'. They were assured the 'vice was not uncommon on certain sections of the front, as were also attacks on wounded men'.[3] He had narrowly evaded prosecution in the military court by being diagnosed with a mental disorder and given a medical discharge. It would transpire the attacks by the soldier had not been sexually motivated but he had been caught in the act of biting the recently deceased and the wounded. He had even bitten the cousin who visited him on the neck, just under the ear, and had drawn blood.

Firth explained that Moriarty (who she calls Z in the text) was firmly of the opinion that neither man was the primary vampire in the case. Moriarty was aware that some Eastern European troops had been sent to serve on the Western Front and among them, he was sure:

---

1. Fortune, Dion, *The Secrets of Dr Taverner* (Douglas, 1926)
2. Fortune, Dion, *Psychic Self-Defence: A Study in Occult Pathology and Criminality* (Rider, 1930)
3. Fortune, Dion, *Psychic Self-Defence: A Study in Occult Pathology and Criminality* (Rider, 1930)

were individuals with the traditional knowledge of Black Magic for which South Eastern Europe has always enjoyed a sinister reputation among occultists. These men getting killed, knew how to avoid going to the Second Death, that is to say, the disintegration of the Astral Body, and maintained themselves in the etheric double by vampiring the wounded.[4]

Moriarty had come to the conclusion that when the older cousin, the soldier, had bitten his regular visitor, the entity within him had transferred to a younger man and could now apparently alternate between the two men.

In the fictional story, Dr Taverner needs to draw out the vampire if he is to vanquish it and calls upon Miss Beryl Wynter, the fiancée of the vampiric Captain Craigie, to assist him. Made aware of the dangers, she still willingly agrees to do 'whatever is necessary'[5] if it stood a chance of helping her beloved Donald. Dr Taverner draws a scalpel out of his pocket case to make a small incision in the skin of her neck, just under the ear, to let out some blood to draw out the vampire like a tethered goat draws out a wolf. It has the desired effect: the predator entity reveals itself and is destroyed by Taverner's psychic powers.

In *Psychic Self-Defence*, Firth explains how Moriarty was always secretive about this method but she believed he resolved the situation by drawing out the entity, psychically 'pinned' it within a magic circle so it could not escape and absorbed the etheric energy of the entity into himself. In so doing, Moriarty deprived the vampiric entity of its means of avoiding the oblivion of the 'Second Death'. Once freed of the entity, both young men went on to make good recoveries.[6]

Violet Firth also relates another case of a woman she only names as 'Miss L' who came to stay at the Grange. In retrospect, an incident shortly after her arrival should have alerted the staff to be on their guard. The horse-drawn carriage that had brought her from Bishop's Stortford to The Grange was pulled by an old and usually placid horse. As 'Miss L' alighted from the carriage, she went to pat the horse and the animal was

---

4. Fortune, Dion, *Psychic Self-Defence: A Study in Occult Pathology and Criminality* (Rider, 1930)
5. Fortune, Dion, *The Secrets of Dr Taverner* (Noel Douglas, 1926)
6. Fortune, Dion, *Psychic Self-Defence: A Study in Occult Pathology and Criminality* (Rider, 1930)

'galvanized into life at her touch as if she had stung him. He threw up his head, backed, snorted and nearly turned the equipage over in the ditch'. Miss L was unphased, and appearing an agreeable person, was welcomed inside. The driver, however, was left aghast and exclaimed that he had never known the horse to behave like that before and viewed Miss L 'with disfavour'.

That night, a number of staff and boarders had suffered nightmares and had unusually disturbed nights. As the staff began to exchange their experiences 'Miss L' became visibly uncomfortable and, turning red, she said 'with much emphasis':

These things should not be discussed, it is most unwelcome.[7]

In deference to her feelings, Violet and others around the table stopped talking about the night's events. As time passed, Miss L's behaviour became more and more odd. She seemed to want to push her attentions onto Violet, who rebuffed her, but one day, when the pair were working in the kitchen together, Miss L came at Violet with a carving knife and was only dissuaded when Violet fended her off with a large saucepan that had been boiling cabbage and Moriarty happened to walk in on the incident. His presence seemed to break the tension; everything calmed down over lunchtime and afterwards, Miss L seemed overcome by an after-reaction from her excitement and had to retire to her room 'prostrated by exhaustion'.[8]

Firth expressed her concerns to Moriarty, and he assured her he would soon have the matter in hand. He then went to the bathroom, grabbed a soap dish, filled it with water from the tap and made 'certain passes' over it. He then dipped his finger in the water and drew a five-pointed star upon the threshold of Miss L's room. There she remained for the next 48 hours until Moriarty fetched her out again.

Another matter that aroused concern was Miss L's reaction to the small silver cross Violet habitually wore, which she had purchased and had actually been blessed by a priest before she came to The Grange.

7. Fortune, Dion, *Psychic Self-Defence: A Study in Occult Pathology and Criminality* (Rider, 1930)
8. Fortune, Dion, *Psychic Self-Defence: A Study in Occult Pathology and Criminality* (Rider, 1930)

On several occasions, Miss L clearly 'could not bear the sight of it' and asked Violet to tuck it away in her frock out of sight.[9]

Further strange things began to occur. Over the following days, the heavy front door of the Grange, which was shut and secured each night by two large bolts that extended across, had the heavy chain removed and the huge lock undone. It was found ajar when staff came down in the morning. Enquiries were made as to who had left it open and why but they elicited no responses. Moriarty said he would deal with the matter and drew the pentagram in blessed water, point to door, outside 'Miss L's' room each night. Moriarty also marked the floor outside his door with a pentagram, point outwards and 'Miss L.' would find any excuse not to enter his room at any time of the day. The front door was not found ajar any more after that. 'Miss L.' left shortly afterwards, exclaiming that she had been 'cured'.[10]

While 'Miss L' was at The Grange, several boarders and staff members began to suffer from what appeared to be severe 'mosquito bites'. They did not observe what had caused the bites. The bites did not become infected but they appeared to bleed freely. Violet recalled waking up one morning to find a patch of blood the size of her hand on her pillow, which had apparently bled from a small puncture wound just behind the angle of her jaw. Not much was said at the time of these incidents by those who suffered them.[11]

When 'Miss L' departed from the Grange, the bites stopped and those who had been bitten eventually spoke about those incidents in conversation. Moriarty had not suffered any bites but on finally hearing of the cases at the Grange, he stated that he had encountered similar incidents before and was convinced it had been the work of a vampire. Violet recorded Moriarty had also commented he had seen cases in Africa:

> where the victim had become so bloodless that it was with difficulty that a specimen of blood could be obtained for examination, for it could hardly be induced to flow from the debilitated tissues. Nothing can be done for such cases by medical science. They are

9. Fortune, Dion, *Psychic Self-Defence: A Study in Occult Pathology and Criminality* (Rider, 1930)
10. Fortune, Dion, *Psychic Self-Defence: A Study in Occult Pathology and Criminality* (Rider, 1930)
11. Fortune, Dion, *Psychic Self-Defence: A Study in Occult Pathology and Criminality* (Rider, 1930)

dying by inches, and yet no organic disease can be demonstrated. Nevertheless, their appearance is that of a person sinking from repeated hemorrages.[12]

I am certain those who had been bitten were also thankful that the feast of blood had been just that and no apparent contagion of the vampire had been passed on with the bites.

Did Marie Fornario experience this or any other terrifying encounters at The Grange? By her own admission, Violet Firth would state how at 'at one time we did a great deal of work together'. Had Marie been bitten or was she one who bravely volunteered to act as bait to draw out a vampiric entity? She had never really travelled since she had been brought to England as a baby, not even with her family as she was growing up, but it should not be forgotten that the conditions of her grandfather's will had not exactly been conducive for travel abroad. Her guardians certainly don't leap out from the pages of the Ling family history as those inclined to foreign holidays either. Marie was now in her twenties. She had had access to her money for years. She could easily have taken a holiday abroad if she so desired. A particularly good time would have been before she took up her studies at The Grange and she had not done so, but between 13 August and 27 August 1921, she suddenly went on a cruise around the Norwegian fjords aboard the SS *Ormuz*.[13]

The 14,167-ton liner *SS Ormuz* and her sister ship *SS Ormonde*, operated by the Orient Line, provided popular pleasure cruises of Norway and its fjords between the months of July and August in the early 1920s. Offering single berth cabins and cabins deluxe for extra comfort, a 13-day 'summer holiday' cruise could be purchased from 25 guineas and upwards.

It would be far from fast-paced; this holiday experience was sedate in the golden age of cruising. The tone is summed up well in the corporate souvenir book *With an Orient Liner through the Fjords of Norway* (1922), which pulled no punches in stating the only people who would be disappointed by the cruise 'are the people who should go to Yarmouth or Blackpool, where there are always entertainers on the sands by day

---

12. Fortune, Dion, *Psychic Self-Defence: A Study in Occult Pathology and Criminality* (Rider, 1930)
13. TNA HO 334-94

and Pierrots on the pier at night. The sort of people who like that sort of thing should keep away from Norway'.[14]

Marie would later record pointedly that she 'slept on board all the time'.[15] Perhaps she wanted to make it clear that she had never strayed far from the liner; maybe she was suffering from seasickness? Or did she require a holiday amongst the placid fjords and the fresh, pure Scandinavian air in an attempt to cleanse herself from *something* sinister and paranormal that she had experienced and wanted to lock herself away in her cabin at night time in the 'land of the midnight sun'?

14. Heywood Hadfield, P., *With an Orient Liner through the Fjords of Norway* (London Stereoscopic, 1922)
15. TNA HO 144-1765-431695

Chapter 6

The Immortal Hour

I have come hither, led by dreams and visions
Fiona MacLeod

On Marie's return from the cruise, she was encouraged by Violet Firth to join the Rosicrucian Order of Alpha et Omega, a splinter group of the elite secret society, The Golden Dawn. Alpha et Omega would no doubt have appealed to Marie Fornario because of its esoteric nature and its worthy membership but the fact that William Sharp, who wrote under the name of Fiona MacLeod, whose writings Marie cherished above all others, had been a member of the original Golden Dawn would undoubtedly added impetus for her to join. Sadly, she would never share ceremonies with Sharp because by the time she came to join, he had been dead for over fifteen years but she would no doubt have felt a little closer to Sharp by following in his footsteps. In the Golden Dawn and Alpha et Omega, members adopted names of sentiment, family motto or literary allusions. Marie Fornario chose Mac Tyler; Mac from her love of the works of Fiona Macleod, and Tyler from her office in Co-Freemasonry, the Outer Guard, otherwise known as the Tyler.

Marie began the process of nationalisation (now known as British citizenship) in April 1922. Her three referees were Ernest Augustus Bongers (41), a colour merchant of 321 High Holborn who lived with his Scottish-born wife Margaret (41), in Purley, Surrey. Bongers had been born in Kentish Town; he was a school friend of Marie's uncle George Duncan Ling, her guardian, and had known Marie since she was a child. John Albert Dennison (49), a consultant mining engineer with The Anglo-Frenche Exploration Co. Ltd., a neighbour who lived with his wife and two grown-up sons on Blanford Road, Reigate and widower William George Lewis (77), a retired civil servant (customs and excise) whose daughter lived with him at Evesham Lodge, Evesham Road in Reigate.

All of her referees were described as being 'of irreproachable character' in the covering letter from James Metcalfe, the Reigate Head Constable. Frederick Beck, one of the partners in the solicitors Neve, Beck & Sons of 21, Lime Street, London EC 3, who were representing Marie in her application, noted in a covering letter:

> The Applicant's education has been entirely British and she is unquestionably of pronounced British sympathies. All her money is invested by the Trustees in British Securities, and it is for these reasons that she is desirous of obtaining naturalization.[1]

Two notices were placed in *The Times* on 28 and 29 April 1922 as per common procedure at the time, announcing Marie was applying for naturalisation asking 'that any person who knows any reason why naturalisation should not be granted should send a written and signed statement of the facts to the Under- Secretary of State, Home Office, London SW1'.

No objections were received and her certificate of British naturalisation was granted on 4 July 1922. Her name changed slightly on the certificate too; Norah, her mother's name, previously Marie's third and final Christian name appears first in order as Marie Norah Emily Edith Fornario. Those who shared membership of her secret society or esoteric connections knew her by her chosen A.O. name of Mac.[2] Her name is also recorded on AO documents as Netta Fornario.[3] On official documents, she signed her name as Marie E. Fornario[4] and following the style popular in the first half of the twentieth century, she would use her middle name of Norah for informal day-to-day transactions with people who had come to know her well enough not to address her as Miss Fornario.

Can you imagine one of your most cherished books on myths and legends by your favourite author and the magical world they introduced to your imagination brought to the stage in a superbly crafted dramatisation? A spectacle of costumes, song and music that recaptured all the magic

---

1. TNA HO 144-1765-431695
2. Fortune, Dion, *Psychic Self-Defence: A Study in Occult Pathology and Criminality* (Rider, 1930)
3. Colquhoun, Ithell, *Sword of Wisdom: MacGregor Mathers and the Golden Dawn* (Spearman, 1975)
4. TNA HO 144-1765-431695

and fantasy of the original book for you? The experience of such a performance can feel like a very personal journey. Such adaptations are rare but it does happen. For Marie Fornario, it was the adaptation of her favourite author, Fiona MacLeod's book *The Immortal Hour*, into an opera of the same name.

The opera was the loving creation of English composer Rutland Boughton, who had been inspired by how Wagner drew upon powerful stories from Germanic heroic legend, Norse sagas, and folklore for inspiration to create his most iconic and popular operas, such as his epic Cycle *Der Ring des Nibelungen*. Wagner's operas were performed amid magnificent spectacles of costume, music, stage sets and powerful use of light that had transcended into a socio-cultural phenomenon through the Bayreuth Festival since the 1870s.

As Wagner had been drawn to Germanic legends, so Boughton was drawn to the Arthurian mythos and where better to found his 'English Bayreuth' than Glastonbury in Somerset. This truly mystical area is steeped in legend. It is a strong candidate for the Isle of Avalon of the stories and it is where King Arthur and Queen Guinevere are said to rest in their tomb before the high altar in Glastonbury abbey church.

By 1911, Boughton and his partner Christina Walshe had moved into a large house called Chalice Well and opened a summer school of music and drama there with the aim of training local people to become the singers, instrumentalists and dancers performing at what would become the Glastonbury Festivals. A national appeal to finance these events and even the construction of a purpose-built concert hall for these performances received the backing of many of those who were the quintessential essence of British classical music and culture. There were the composers – Sir Edward Elgar, Sir Hubert Parry, Sir Granville Bantock, Dame Ethel Smyth, Gustav Holst, Ralph Vaughan Williams and Percy Grainger, who all publicly endorsed the venture as did conductors Henry Wood, Eugene Goossens and Thomas Beecham. Many others also gave their support, such as novelist and playwright John Galsworthy, the influential actor and director Gordon Craig and the playwright, critic and man of letters, George Bernard Shaw.

The first opera to be performed was not to be the projected Arthurian Cycle, but instead, it would be Boughton's new choral drama based on

Fiona MacLeod's play *The Immortal Hour*. Boughton's partner Christina Walshe was half Irish by birth. She was a passionate supporter of the 'Celtic revival' and she had been influential in the encouragement of Boughton's interest in the myths, legendary tales and folk songs of Ireland and Scotland.

The Immortal Hour, which would become Boughton's most enduring work, is a retelling of the Gaelic legend of the *Sidhe* folk (the model for Tolkien's elves), based on the Irish story *Tochmarc Étaíne*, the 'Wooing of Etain'. The story begins with Etain, a young waif, wandering a wood. She was of the faery folk, but chose to be mortal so she 'would know the mortal love for which men die'.

As she leaves the scene, Eochaid, the poet-king enters. He is also walking in the forest and he encounters Dalua, the Faery Fool whose touch brings madness or death to man. Eochaidh tells Dalua of his quest for 'The Immortal Hour – the joy beyond all mortal joy, the beauty of all beauty'. Dalua convinces him this can be found but it only resides in love – not love that knows desire but the love which is peace. Before the young king departs, Dalua lays his hand upon him. While still in the woods a storm erupts and Eochaidh seeks shelter in a peasant's cottage, inside he finds Etain standing by the fire doing the same. As in all good faerie tales, they fall in love, but there is a far-away look in Etain's eyes. There is faery singing which only she can hear …

The pair marry, and a year after Etain became his queen, they hold a great celebration attended by many noble guests including warriors and druids. Etain gets that look in her eyes again during the celebration, she can hear the Faery Song again and tiring, she leaves the court. Eochaidh is left feeling uneasy as a stranger joins the celebration who asks that he may touch the queen's hand with his lips and sing her a song he has made.

Eochaidh, bound by a hasty promise to a guest, agrees and sends for Etain. The song the stranger sings is The Faery Song and from the moment he begins to sing it, Etain only has eyes for the stranger. The stranger is, in fact, Prince Midir of her own faery folk and he draws Etain out into the night with him and the pair go off together into the darkness. Eochaidh is broken by this and laments the futility of his dreams. As Eochaidh laments, Dalua appears again and having wrought madness on the king, he now bestows death upon him.

It was a great story that lent itself well to the operatic narrative. With the backing of so many influential figures, all was ready to go with the festival but it had been planned for August 1914, the same month that the First World War broke out. With the storm clouds of war gathering, people had held onto their money and funds had not been sufficient to build the theatre but the festival performances still went ahead in Glastonbury's Assembly Rooms. There was a grand piano instead of an orchestra and a chorus and staff drawn mostly from local people but they were filled with enthusiasm and gave their all.

Christina Walshe designed striking costumes for the performances but unable to afford the intended sets, she came up with the innovative concept of using the chorus as 'living scenery' whereby they created images such as waves breaking on castle walls through the medium of mime or dance. These performances drew attention and acclaim from London critics from national newspapers. Even George Bernard Shaw was moved to compare it favourably to Bayreuth. Audiences soon comprised many who had made 'pilgrimages' from London. Indeed, theatregoers would soon come from all over the country to witness the spectacle each year.

Michael Scott Rohan commented in his excellent retrospective on the first Glastonbury Festivals:

There was nothing else like it in Britain, and never really had been – a vivid, exciting experimental nexus to compete with European institutions[5]

After the end of the war in 1918, the festival would prove to be the launch of a theatrical phenomenon. As Rohan pointed out:

'The Immortal Hour,' the epitome of 'Celtic Twilight', had come to embody Glastonbury's idealistic, quasi-mystical ambience. Elgar called it 'a work of genius'; Dame Ethel Smyth was 'enchanted by it', and Shaw and any number of other musical luminaries praised it. Vaughan Williams said that in any other country 'it would have been in the repertoire years ago'[6]

---

5. *Classical Music, BBC Music Magazine* (online) 22 June 2022
6. *Classical Music, BBC Music Magazine* (online) 22 June 2022

In 1921, actor-manager Sir Barry Jackson staged *The Immortal Hour* at The Repertory Theatre in Birmingham with Gwen Ffrangcon-Davies in the lead role of Etain. The popularity of the show boded well and Jackson took it to London, where the opera was an incredible success. Gwen Ffrangcon-Davies' performance was truly captivating. In fact, the whole show seemed to cast its own spell over audiences that drew people back to experience it again and again. *The Immortal Hour* still retains the record for continuous opera performances with a run of 221, and a further 160 the following year.[7]

Gwen Ffrangcon-Davies went on to have one of the longest acting careers in theatre, film and television; she performed with some of the biggest theatrical names in the Twentieth Century and even appeared in the Hammer classics *The Witches* (1966) and *The Devil Rides Out* (1968). Still performing well into her later life, Gwen was made a Dame in 1991 when she was aged 100. Interviewed in 1983, after reminiscing about her introduction to the theatrical world and Dame Ellen Terry, she recalled *The Immortal Hour* and words failed her when trying to describe quite what a phenomenon it was:

> It was a cult. People absolutely … I suppose they were glad to see something of beauty and hope and removal from the gross material world and into the land of heart's desire and of the ever young, the beauty, and the beauty of the music. The strangeness of the atmosphere after the filth and dreadfulness four years of misery and agony of the trenches and the war. Perhaps that had something to do with it …

Marie Fornario was one of those captured by the magic of the show. She would return to see it many times and was so enamoured by the opera she would write an eloquent commentary under her spiritual name of Mac Tyler: *The Immortal Hour, An Interpretation of the play* published by Frederick Newman, London in a 19-page booklet in 1923. It remains one of the few examples of Marie's known writings to survive and it is

7. *Classical Music, BBC Music Magazine* (online) 22 June 2022

reproduced in its entirety in Appendix 2. In the body of this book, I share but an excerpt. I particularly like her introductory comments:

> During the course of some three and twenty performances of "The Immortal Hour", the writer of this booklet has gained much amusement from the comments of the audience, yet, if various remarks overheard on such occasions have enlivened the interval between the two acts with flashes of humour, (mostly unconscious on the part of the speakers), they also provided matter for considerable reflection.
>
> Visitors to the Regent Theatre may be roughly classified as follows; students of mysticism and folk-lore who are able to understand the great truths concealed behind this gossamer curtain of faery; (a small clan, but they come frequently and every time discover some new aspect of illuminating significance), a large number of people who think the play beautiful but sad; and many for whom the whole drama is so elusive and incomprehensible that they irritably demand of each other "what on earth the fellow can be getting at," and are frankly bored: and there is a fourth class who, while keenly appreciating the artistic beauty of the performance, also sense the existence of a deeper meaning, but are hopelessly baffled by their inability to interpret the intricate symbolism employed…

Marie was clearly in her element, but sadly, nothing lasts forever and some things end a lot sooner than we hope.

Chapter 7

The Green Ray

There are moments when the soul takes wings:
what it has to remember, it remembers: what it loves,
it loves still more: what it longs for, to that it flies.
Fiona MacLeod

Heacham is a delightful coastal village in West Norfolk that lies around three miles from Hunstanton and 14 miles from King's Lynn. It has fine dunes dotted with slat-boarded wooden beach huts and bungalows along its sand dunes that sway with marrams in gentle breezes on fine days. Its wide-open beaches on the east banks of The Wash are one of the few places in eastern England where the sun can appear to set over the sea rather than the land.

In the 1920s, Heacham was the quieter option to bustling Hunstanton for a seaside holiday and the ideal place for a day trip out by car, train, motorcycle or bicycle with a cup of tea and a bun at Pratt's Tea Room when staying in the west of the county. So, when Theodore Moriarty was staying at The Duke's Head Hotel, which overlooks the historic Tuesday Market Place in King's Lynn on Saturday, 18 August 1923, it comes as no surprise that he would be tempted to visit Heacham. Sadly, no clues as to why he was visiting West Norfolk have been found to date, whether he was visiting friends, investigating a case or having a break away on his own.

It has been suggested he might have been visiting members of the Allen family at Cockley Cley Hall but that is some 18 miles away inland from Lynn and, if he did not stay at the Hall itself, The George Hotel in the nearby market town of Swaffham would have been a lot more convenient. All we know, drawn from newspaper reports, is that Moriarty was taken ill at Heacham. He was attended by a doctor who had advised him that he should return to the Duke's Head at King's Lynn where he had been staying and rest. Moriarty dropped dead at the hotel the same evening; his lifeless body was found by fellow guest Diana Nicholls.

Local GP, Dr Philip Sydney Marshall MRCS, who lived at The Hollies in nearby Snettisham, certified the cause of death as *Angina Pectoris*. The condition was often a symptom of coronary artery disease. In laymen's terms, Moriarty died of a heart attack. It had not been a month since Moriarty had celebrated his fiftieth birthday. He did not appear to have been in failing health, nor was he obese or a habitual smoker. Local authorities seemed quite happy with the conclusion of Dr Marshall; there was no suspicion of foul play so no inquest was ordered. There were, however, rumblings in the occult world that something or someone had killed him by a 'psychic attack'. Moriarty had battled enough dark forces in his time to draw such a reprisal, or perhaps if someone believed he had appropriated secrets from one secret order to use in the new societies he established, he could have been cursed. For example, anyone who broke The Golden Dawn's oath of silence, it was claimed, would 'fall dead or paralysed as if blasted by lightning'.[1]

Another far more corporeal matter is the age shown on his death certificate. Moriarty's birth certificate exists and it clearly states his date of birth as 27 July 1873, so it is curious that his death certificate should state his age as 58. It also shows his rank or profession as 'Medical Practitioner' and his home address is recorded as 26 Sinclair Road, London W14, where he also held the meetings of his Co-Masonic Lodge.

Sadly, a search of online newspapers and even contemporary editions of *The Occult Review* does not yield any obituary for Moriarty nor any immediately apparent report of a funeral or memorial service. Wondering if Moriarty was given a local burial to avoid the expense of transporting his body to another location, a search of the burial and cremation records of the cemeteries that the Borough Council of King's Lynn and West Norfolk is responsible for, revealed no trace of him.

So, what happened to Moriarty's body, at least for the time being, remains a mystery, just like that of his namesake, who disappeared after tumbling into the Reichenbach Falls while grappling with Sherlock Holmes in *The Final Problem* (1893). The assumption readers were left

---

1. Wilson, Richard, *Scotland's Unsolved Mysteries*, (Hale, Revised Edition 1995)

with was that both of them had died as a result of the fall but neither of their bodies were recovered. Doyle brought Holmes back but not Moriarty, leaving readers wondering if he would one day return too. I think Theodore William Carte Moriarty would have liked that. Or, he undoubtedly had friends who looked out for him and would ensure if he had suffered death as the result of a curse in this world, they would do all they could to protect him in the next and ensure his remains in this world were handled, buried or cremated and scattered with appropriate caution.

After Moriarty's death, the dynamic of The Grange changed. Violet Firth no longer worked there and Marie moved out and went to live in Eastbourne, the seaside town she knew well. She made her new home in a one-bedroom flat at 15 Bolton Road, a Victorian terraced hall entrance residence, not far from Grand Parade, that had been divided into apartments for gentlefolk. Set just far away enough from the seafront to be sedate, Bolton Road was one of the places in the town where bath chairs could be hired for perambulations to take the health-giving air of the resort. Marie shared occupancy of 15 Bolton Road with Charlotte Louise and Arthur Mark (known as Mark) Lickfold, and sisters Frances Madeline and Eleanor Grace Stabb. All of whom lived off private means, most likely inherited money.

In 1924, Violet Firth and Charles Loveday formed The Fraternity of Inner Light (later renamed The Society of Inner Light) as 'an Outer Court' to the Golden Dawn. Firth created its temple and headquarters at 3 Queensborough Terrace, a fine Georgian three-storey, hall entrance terraced house, with steps up and columns at its door, in Bayswater, London. Marie Fornario also left Alpha et Omega and was initiated into the Inner Light in 1925.

Prospective initiates were trained in the workings of the society by means of correspondence courses and upon successful completion of the course, aspirants would be initiated into the Lesser Mysteries that were roughly equivalent to those of the Outer Order of the Golden Dawn. They could then progress through further study onto Greater Mysteries that equated to the workings of the old Inner Order of the Rosicrucian *Rosae Rubae et Aureae Crucis* (Membership of Ruby Rose and Golden Cross was only open to Master Freemasons). These sacred workings were much extolled by Moriarty but they were also those used by the

Golden Dawn. Moina Mathers, High Priestess of The Golden Dawn order that Firth had belonged to, was clearly displeased with Violet for using unchanged versions of Golden Dawn rituals for her Inner Light ceremonies. Much to Mather's consternation, Violet was betraying some of the secrets she had sworn to safeguard and expelled her, alleging that she had the 'wrong signs in her aura'.

Violet was always selective but keen to recruit new initiates. Bayswater appears to have been a very suitable area to find new members. Independent of Violet, a Fellowship Club was established at nearby Lancaster Gate in 1925. A report in the local newspaper explained the ethos of the group, which reflects the growing interest in more esoteric matters among the educated public at that time:

> Most of us at the present time are ever ready to welcome new ideas, new schools of thought. The strenuosity of modern life demands it. We must have some centre where, forgetting the whirl and turmoil of present-day existence, we can quietly foregather, either for pleasant social intercourse or for the discussion of those more urgent and compelling problems of life itself.
>
> Such a very obvious need is supplied by the Fellowship Club, 52, Lancaster Gate, where for a very modest annual subscription one can become a member of the Club, and be initiated into the 'mysteries' of the very latest modern school of thought, comprising such world-wide subjects as Theosophy Occultism, Healing and Meditation, Philosophy, together with the enjoyment of many delightful musical and dramatic recitals at frequent intervals.[2]

The meetings of the Fellowship Club were held in the handsomely decorated drawing room of Lancaster Gate. As those attending evening lectures gathered, the sense of occasion was complimented by tasteful musical accompaniment until the speaker was introduced. Violet would speak for the club on a number of occasions and despite being the author of the Dr Taverner serial and book between 1925 and 1927, she always spoke under her own name rather than using Dion Fortune. Violet's talks

---

2. *Bayswater Chronicle*, 28 March 1925

were always very well attended and were both advertised and reported in some detail in the *Bayswater Chronicle*. Violet made her first presentation, 'An Account of Some Occult Experiences' on the evening of Wednesday, 25 March 1925. The subsequent newspaper report not only provides us with an insight into what she spoke about but also records something of how Violet appeared to her audience:

> The lecturer, fair and exceedingly handsome and a true daughter of Yorkshire, said she was born in the particular part of that county which had been invaded by the Vikings of old. These ancient people were well known to possess certain occult powers. She owed her first occult experience to the fact that she was born in a haunted house. The 'ghost' was a very substantial one, and "bumped" about the house, dropping things on the floor and making a tremendous noise as he came and went. But she contrived to sleep peacefully through it all.

After recounting a number of her occult experiences and speaking candidly about her personal journey of discovery (The complete article is reproduced as Appendix 2 of this book), she concludes with these thoughts:

> Those who desired to obtain a knowledge of the occult must strive to raise consciousness to a higher plane, at the same time bringing down the spiritual forces to a lower level. This achieved, they became real – apparent. But at all times a knowledge of occult powers must be safeguarded by a spiritual outlook.[3]

The year 1926 was to be one of unsettling change for Marie. She would move houses in Eastbourne. The exact dynamic between the people she had been living with on Bolton Road is not recorded but when she moved to her new address at 15 Blackwater Road, Eastbourne, her fellow residents, the Lickfolds and Frances Stabb, are also recorded as residing there.

Violet, writing under the name of Dion Fortune, would have *The Secrets of Dr Taverner* published in book form for the first time in 1926, and

---

3. *Bayswater Chronicle*, 28 March 1925

Marie and Violet would end their association. One can but wonder if Marie had not read the original serialised stories in *The Royal Magazine* but saw a copy of the published book and spotted something within the pages that struck her as a little too close to home to be in general publication, even with the names changed and took offence?

Firth would claim their friendship ended after an incident that occurred at Pentecost on 23 May 1926. The Society of Inner Light was conducting a spiritual ritual at an old orchard they had purchased at the foot of Glastonbury Tor. Members were exhilarated and left with a feeling of ecstasy running through them. Norah believed the experience was a direct result of a messenger from the elemental kingdoms. In her book *Psychic Self Defence* (1930), Violet would recall:

Some three years before her [*Marie's*] death we went our separate ways and lost sight of each other. She was ... of unusual intellectual calibre, and was especially interested in the Green Ray elemental contacts; too much interested in them for my peace of mind, and I became nervous and refused to co-operate with her. I do not object to reasonable risks, in fact one cannot expect to achieve anything worthwhile in life if one will not take risks, but it appeared to me that 'Mac' as we called her, was going to be in very deep waters, even when I knew her, and that there was certain to be trouble sooner or later.[4]

Dion Fortune's biographer, Gareth Knight, author of *Dion Fortune & the Inner Light* (Thoth 2000), explained the Green Ray in these terms:

The three major strands to the Western Mystery Tradition, using the colour symbolism popular when the Society of the Inner Light was first founded, were called the Green Ray, the Orange Ray and the Purple Ray.

The Green Ray consists of the nature contacts in the broadest sense, and encapsulates most mythopoeic formulations relating to nature and to the Earth, including Elemental and Faery traditions. The Orange Ray describes the study of symbolism and its manipulation

---

4. Fortune, Dion, *Psychic Self-Defence: A Study in Occult Pathology and Criminality* (Rider, 1930)

in ceremonial or visualised forms, frequently in terms of the Tree of Life of the Qabalah. The Purple Ray denotes religious mysticism, a direct approach to the spirit, and the devotional way usually expressed in the West in Christian terms.[5]

Sadly, The Grange at Bishop's Stortford never really recovered after the death of Moriarty. By 1926, the days of the educational establishment as an educational centre for the Science, Arts and Crafts Association were numbered. Gwen Stafford-Allen Fornario moved out and went to live at 48 Hanover Gate Mansions, Westminster, London. The sale of the property was advertised in *Country Life on* Saturday, 26 February 1927. Around this time, Marie took the plunge, left Eastbourne behind her and moved to a flat in a house on Bushwood Road, Kew, Richmond, Surrey, near Kew Green and the famous Royal Botanic Gardens.

Marie's manner of dress raised a few eyebrows in the prim and proper London suburb. One report would state: 'She favoured an extraordinary dress of Indian shawls and wore nothing on her head'.[6] Marie also began to use the psychic skills she had developed under the tutelage of Moriarty, often working through trance and telepathy. Marie's housekeeper and cook, Mrs Mabel Florence Varney, (wife of Metropolitan Police Constable Samuel Varney, who was serving in the 'Y' Division in Richmond), who attended her in the afternoons, would recall:

Miss Fornario was always healing people, by telepathy. If people would not let her heal them she would moan and cry piteously but she was otherwise cheerful and happy. … She would shut herself up in her room, put blankets over her feet and a large white sheet over her head and shoulders. Covered in this way, she would remain for hours and sometimes days together and tell me afterwards that she had healed people by telepathy and had seen extraordinary visions. She told me that she had had visions and spoken to people by telepathy. Several times she said she had been to the 'far beyond' and had come back to life after spending some time in another world. When I suffered from headaches she would put her lovely

---

5. http://garethknight.blogspot.com/2015/10/dion-fortune-and-three-fold-way.html
6. *Daily Express,* 27 November 1929

white hands on my forehead and cure me. She had extraordinary healing powers ...[7]

On another occasion I found her in bed with a sheet drawn up over her head. She asked me not to disturb her as she was in deep thought. She stayed in bed for fourteen days, eating nothing and drinking only orange juice. She often fasted, believing that it helped her spiritual nature.[8]

She absorbed herself in spiritualism and telepathy and mysticism and claimed to have extraordinary visions of other worlds ... On one occasion she said she would fast for 40 days but was persuaded to give it up after a fortnight. Miss Fornario went off into trances and would remain in that condition for hours ... She went into long spells of silence and fasted to develop her healing arts. She was a woman with intellectual gifts and believed she could get into telepathic contact with people in all parts of the world. She had a certain amount of magnetic personality, which overawed women of weaker character.[9]

Mrs Varney would also provide some of the few insights into Marie's personality and lifestyle in interviews she gave to the press:

She dressed in a long cape-like garment she made herself and never wore a hat. Several times she said she had been to the 'far beyond' and had come back to life after spending some time in another world.[10]

I had to do everything for her – even put her to bed at night and serve her meals for her. She was like a child. Sometimes friends would come and help her in her seances, but more often she would work quite alone.[11]

The only food Miss Fornario would eat was minced nuts, grated cheese and potatoes. She was such a vegetarian that she insisted on bringing up her cat as a vegetarian, but the cat died.[12]

---

7. *Richmond Herald*, 30 November 1929
8. *Daily Express*, 27 November 1929
9. *London Daily Chronicle*, Wednesday 27 November 1929
10. *The Scotsman*, 27 November 1929
11. *Richmond Herald*, 30 November 1929
12. *Daily Express*, 27 November 1929

Mortlake Road neighbour, Robert Wright, recalled Marie frequently wore a Victorian dress of many colours when she went walking in the district, adding: 'She was a beautiful woman with her luminous dark eyes and jet-black hair, her skin was very clear, her voice was cultured and her manner gentle'.[13]

Another person only described in the press as 'a friend' of Miss Fornario clearly did not understand Marie or her lifestyle but her recollections offer a clue as to why she moved out (or had been asked to leave) her Bushwood Road flat to another on Mortlake Road:

> A family living in a flat below Miss Fornario's had had to leave because of her peculiar ways. She joined every spiritualistic and advanced religious society in London. If anyone tried to remonstrate with her she swept them aside with quotations and alleged experiences she had. A society which takes an interest in lonely women tried to help her, but they were unable to do anything. She said she cured one or two women by putting her hands on their heads.[14]

The same 'friend' went on to add, 'Part of her life had been spent in a mental home'[15] but no reference to this appears on the papers relating to her nationalisation nor does a search of online databases of admission registers for Lunatic Asylums yield any evidence of this being the case. If it was not just a derisory remark, the tenor of other comments made by the 'friend' suggests it was their interpretation of a mention Marie may have made about her time at The Grange.

In July 1928, Marie Fornario had her first article published in *The Occult Review* under her spiritual name of Mac Tyler. The article titled *The Use of Imagination in Art, Science and Business* was another fascinating and eloquent discussion and it is published in entirety in Appendix 3. Marie's article shared the same edition as *The Haunter and the Haunted* by A Ghost, *The Basis of Witchcraft* by Colin Still and *Touchstone* by Edward Arthur Waite, the Occultist and author of such tomes as *The Real History of the Rosicrucians* (1887), *The Book of Black Magic and Pacts* (1898) and

---

13. *Daily News,* 28 November 1929
14. *London Daily Chronicle,* Wednesday 27 November 1929
15. *London Daily Chronicle,* Wednesday 27 November 1929

The Book of Ceremonial Magic (1913). Waite had also been a member of The Golden Dawn and inspired fellow GD Temple member the artist Pamela 'Pixie' Colman Smith to take a deep interest in Arthurian legend and the quest for the Holy Grail. Waite and Pixie created one of the most popular tarot cards of the twentieth century, first published by William Rider & Son in 1909.

Pixie (a nickname bestowed upon her by actress Ellen Terry) had worked with the Lyceum Theatre company and got to know the theatre's acting manager, Bram Stoker, the author of *Dracula*. She would provide the illustrations for what would prove to be Stoker's last novel, *The Lair of the White Worm* (1911) and would create artwork for the illustrated verses for her friend and another Golden Dawn member, W B Yeats. Pixie and Marie both shared a great interest in the esoteric and faerie folk; they even dressed similarly in Bohemian style. Pixie had also lost both of her parents by the age of 21.

Swallows and Amazons author Arthur Ransome knew Pixie when she was living in Chelsea and wrote in *Bohemia in London* (1907) of how she enraptured audiences dressed in her clothes of many colours, telling stories in candlelit rooms filled with the smoke and pungent aroma created by incense burning in its urn:

She told them in an old dialect, in a manner of her own. Fastening a strip of ruddy tow about her head so that it mingled with her own black hair, she flopped down on the floor behind a couple of lighted candles and, after a little introductory song that she had learned from a Jamaican nurse, told story after story, illustrating them with the help of wooden toys that she had made herself. She told them with such precision of phrasing that those who came often to listen soon had them by heart and would interrupt her like children when, in a single word, she went astray. To hear her was to be carried back to the primitive days of storytelling and to understand, a little, how it was that the stories of the old minstrels were handed on from man to man.[16]

In her 1908 article *Should the Art Student Think?*, Pixie offers the advice: 'Use your wits, use your eyes. Perhaps you use your physical eyes too much and only see the mask. Find your eyes within, look for the door

---

16. Ransome, Arthur, *Bohemia in London* (Chapman & Hall, 1907)

in the unknown country.' In the feature '*A Painter Who Sees Fairies*', M. Irwin MacDonald describes her vividly:

> Pamela Colman Smith is so naturally a mystic that she has but little intellectual interest in mysticism. From childhood she has had the gift of second sight ... and she believes in what she sees as simply and implicitly as they do. She never thinks of this power as clairvoyance, or exploits it as such, but uses it precisely as she does the senses and faculties which are common to all. In temperament and personality she is much an anachronism as was William Morris, for like him she belongs to an earlier age ...[17]

Above all, she was blessed with the ability to see clearly the 'invisible world':

> She learned to distinguish the elementals of the earth, air, fire and water – the gnomes, goblins, wraiths, leprechauns, pixies, salamanders and people of the sea. But most often in Ireland she saw the Sidhe, the invisible children of Dana ...

By the 1920s, Pixie had converted to Catholicism and was living in Cornwall and only came to London occasionally but her love of Arthurian legend, and her fascination with the Holy Grail quest and faerie folk never left her. A few postcards with only the briefest messages from Marie to Pixie are known to exist. The messages are so brief that they offer no real indication of the extent or nature of their friendship but they are certainly cordial, showing that the pair did meet and enjoyed conversations about the fae.

Marie became acquainted with other like-minded people through the circle of *Occult Review* and allied writers, among them were Richard and Iona Cammell. Richard would become joint editor of *The Atlantis Quarterly* with fellow occult researcher and author Lewis Spence in 1932. Cammell would write one of the first biographies of 'The Beast 666' *Aleister Crowley: The Man, The Mage, The Poet*, first published in

---

17. *The Craftsman*, Volume XXIII No. 1 October 1912

1951. His wife, Iona Katherine MacDonald Cammell, was Scottish by birth and a dealer in Scottish tweeds. She had a great love of the mystical Hebridean Island of Iona, especially its folklore and legends.

Iona was good friends with the folklorist Miss Lucy Bruce, who regularly visited the island of Iona and would build a second home there between Traigh Bhan and Iona Abbey that she would name Grianan (Scottish Gaelic for House of the Sun) in 1930. Most certainly a kindred spirit of Marie, Lucy not only believed in faerie folk, she firmly believed she was in contact with the *Sidhe* resident on Iona and frequently saw them on the island. Her friend, the Scottish writer and folklorist Alasdair Alpin MacGregor, wrote of her in *The Ghost Book* (1955):

> Miss Lucy Bruce, who spends a good deal of the year at Grianan, her home on the island, and who perhaps knows its arcana more intimately than anybody living, tells me that the other day, when walking with a Norwegian friend at the north-west extremity of the island, the friend suddenly beheld a troop of the Little People. They stood about a foot in stature; and they asked her for a blessing, which she promptly gave them. That evening she saw them again, in the Faery Room at Grianan. As as sign that they had accepted Christianity, they had brought with them a little Cross fashioned out of twigs and leaves.[18]

Lucy Bruce was an active member of the Fairy Investigation Society (FIS) in the 1930s. She would also be part of the FIS revival in the post-war years when membership also included Walt Disney and Air Chief Marshal Sir Hugh Dowding, the man who had been head of RAF Fighter Command during The Battle of Britain in 1940. The accounts of the faerie folk Miss Bruce claims she and others witnessed on Iona stretch the bounds of belief but it matters not if we believe in the paranormal and occult or not in understanding this case. What does matter is how vehemently Marie Fornario and anyone potentially involved in her untimely death believed in it, which could prove to be the key that unlocks this case.

---

18. Alasdair Alpin MacGregor, *The Ghost Book* (Hale, 1955)

Lucy would have undoubtedly shared the remarkable stories of her encounters with faery folk on Iona with Marie but I don't think that was the only draw. The Green Ray had also been the title and theme of the book *Le Rayon-Vert* by Jules Verne, first published in 1882.

Verne weaves a tale around the mythical Scottish legend of the Green Ray that only appears when the sun passes the horizon over the sea, when the sky is clear. Sir Arthur Conan Doyle told of how he saw it for himself in a letter to the Editor of *Occult Review* published in October 1922:

Dear Sir, – I have twice seen the Green Ray, once in the Mediterranean and once in the Atlantic. One needs a perfectly clear sunset without a trace of haze. Then just as the upper rim vanishes – or possibly a second later – there rises what is more like a puff of green smoke than anything else I can describe. I presume that it is an effect of refraction from the light shining through the curve of water, but I have never heard any scientific explanation.

According to Verne's version of the legend, the person viewing the Green Ray, is granted the ability to see into their own heart and read the hearts of others. Verne set the denouement of his story on Iona too, with good reason. The views across the sea and ocean around the island afford spectacular views of sunrise and sunset, offering a good chance of seeing the Green Ray for real.

Marie would travel alone when she first visited Iona in August 1928.[19] She then moved to 73 Mortlake Road, Kew, Richmond, Surrey, in 1929 but after just two months on Mortlake Road Marie, set off again for Iona with plans to stay for the winter. The question will always be why did Marie return to Iona again so quickly? Was it really just to go and contemplate a book she was planning to write or was there something far darker that she was trying to escape?

---

19. *Richmond Herald*, 30 November 1929

Chapter 8

The Island of Myths and Legends

Man is born to believe, and if no church comes forward with its title deeds of truth, sustained in the traditions of sacred ages and by the convictions of countless generations, to guide him, he will find altars and idols in his heart and in his own imagination.

Benjamin Disraeli

The island of Iona is found among the Inner Hebrides off the west coast of Scotland. It is approximately three miles long, is less than one and a half miles wide and has had a population of fewer than 200 permanent residents for at least the last 200 years. By many standards, Iona is remote, but fortunately, Marie Fornario was living in what would be looked back upon as a golden age of railway travel when pride was taken in running trains to time and the experience of those travelling by train was made as pleasurable as possible, especially for those who travelled first class, with comfy seats, attentive, smartly uniformed staff and fine carriage decor. It really would have felt like luxury travel.

Well-to-do families would book accommodation on Iona for weeks or even a month or two over the summer and would usually take at least one of their maids or a maid and a nanny for their children with them. It was not unknown for the luggage of such families to consist of over thirty cases, trunks, crates and packages. The Service family who hired Traighmòr in the summer season for many years in the 1920s even took their piano with them. The arrival of the large crate containing it being manhandled from the SS *Dunara Castle* onto the ship-to-shore landing boat and its arrival on the island was quite an annual event.

Each item of luggage would have a railway luggage label affixed to it that stated its station of destination. Once the baggage arrived at the station, the porters would pick up, load and unload the baggage from the train. Travelling from her home at Kew, it is highly likely Marie would have travelled to Scotland from King's Cross station by one of the most famous trains of its day – the legendary Flying Scotsman, the flagship of the London & North Eastern Railway. The Flying Scotsman left the station every weekday at 10.00 am on the dot to make a non-stop journey of 392 miles from King's Cross to Edinburgh in 8 hours and 3 minutes. This train soon became renowned for its speed and in 1934, it would become the first steam locomotive to be officially authenticated, reaching the speed of 100 mph.

The cautious traveller would count their luggage when they arrived at Edinburgh station and then change trains for the coastal town of Oban in Argyll and Bute. The traveller would then need to travel by either a MacBrayne's steamer to Iona that would leave from the North Pier in Oban every day of the week except Sunday. Or catch the ferry from Oban across the Sound of Mull to the Isle of Mull, cross the island and catch another ferry over to Iona. The ferries did not run on a Sunday either.

The old *MacDonald's Guide to Staffa, Iona and the Isle of Mull* promises, 'A trip to Iona and Staffa is a memory for a lifetime, from the riches of which even the accompaniment of dull skies and rough seas should not detract'. Speaking as one with the heart of a Norfolk man but the sea-legs of Nelson (he suffered from terrible sea sickness), I think it only fair to warn potential visitors that a few pages further on in the guide, it cautions:

> The Sound of Mull is one of the most striking coasts which the Hebrides affords to the traveller. In fine weather a grander, more impressive scene, both from its natural beauties and associations with ancient history and traditions, can hardly be imagined. When the day is stormy, the passage is somewhat rough, so that in unsettled weather a stranger, if not much accustomed to the sea, may sometimes add to other sensations excited …[1]

Once departed from Oban and mainland Scotland for the islands of the Hebrides, the traveller passes through an area of outstanding beauty, of coastline, caves, mountains and castles. Here can be found some of the most remarkable legends anywhere and every island has its stories. Even

---

1. *MacDonald's Guide to Staffa, Iona and Island of Mull* (Hugh MacDonald, Oban n.d.)

at the outset, as the steamer departs Oban pier on its way to the north entrance of Kerra Sound and the Firth of Lorn, on the right is the Dog Stone, where the legendary warrior Fingal tethered his dog Bran when he visited Lorn.

Then as the steamer passes the Lismore Lighthouse, there is Lady Rock nearby where, in the sixteenth century, Lauchlan Catenach MacLean of Duart Castle, who believed or claimed to believe his wife Catherine Campbell, daughter of the Earl of Argyll, had attempted to poison him, abandoned her on the rock at low water. He knew full well that as the tide rose, it would engulf the rock and the poor woman would drown … without a mark of violence upon her.

Once he was sure his evil intent had been achieved, MacLean travelled to the home of her kin at Inverary in deep mourning to tell them she had mysteriously disappeared. He was, however, astonished to find the wife he had tried to kill already there. Her plaintive cries for help had been heard by a fisherman who had come to her rescue and she had fled home and told all. In one version of the story, MacLean was slain before he left the Campbells; in another, he fled in shame but he was tracked down by one of Catherine's brothers to Edinburgh where vengeance was served as he stabbed MacLean to death in 1523. As an aside, it would be the same clan Campbell who committed the infamous massacre of the MacDonalds at Glencoe in 1692. Tragically, the bloody stain of battle, slayings, feuds and murder marked the highlands for many a year.

Those catching the ferries across from Oban to Iona in the 1920s would land then as now at Craignure on Mull. Those with small amounts of baggage could catch the bus that made the scenic 37-mile run across the island once a day. Those like Marie who were travelling with larger amounts of luggage would need to hire cars or horse-drawn carts to transport them and their luggage to Fionnphort to catch the ferry to Iona.

Mull, the second largest island of the Inner Hebrides (second to Skye), has been known since antiquity as 'The Island of Gloom', supposedly because of the fogs that often cloaks its landscape. According to legend, Mull was inhabited by 'a race of witches', some of whom worked curses and malevolence upon people using clay or wax images that they would prick or punch to torment those who the figure represented.

Not all of the witches worked for entirely dark purposes. A popular Highland legend tells of one of their number, a woman known as Doideag Mhuileach, who, when she heard of the approach of the Spanish Armada in 1588 brewed up a cataclysmic storm at sea. She then took a clay image of a ship to the sea shore, placed it on the water and every time it sank so did another man-o'-war of the Armada. Witches lingered for centuries on Mull and in the Highlands. The last witch to be tried and executed for witchcraft in Britain was a certain Janet Horne, who was executed and 'purified' by the fire by being burned at the stake at Dornoch in Sutherland in 1727.

Cattle have been a farming staple in the Hebrides since time immemorial, and according to the chronicles of Adomnán the Prior of Iona in the seventh and early eighth centuries, a local belief held: 'Where there is a cow, there will be a woman. And where there is a woman, there will be mischief'. In this context, 'mischief' could mean anything from discord and jealousy to witchcraft and probably inferred a combination of all three. In Hebridean folklore, witches were known to find it difficult to cross water unless transported by others (another folkloric reason why women are not permitted on fishing boats), so Columba took no chances and banished all women from Iona to the island of Eilean-nam-Ban, (The Women's Island), just off the coast of Mull near Fionnphort.

For visitors in the 1920s and today, a small ferry crosses the one-and-a-half miles of beautiful turquoise waters of the Sound of Iona to Iona. At least this is how they look on a fine, sunny spring and summer day; weather conditions are subject to change, sometimes at quite short notice. In the Hebrides, the winds can blow hard and gale force, storms can roll in and calm seas turn to crashing waves.

On a fine day when the wide-open sky is cloudless and fades from azure to navy blue, Iona can be clearly seen across the Sound. It appears a lush, green island and indeed, its green areas are rich in grass, clover, thyme and heather. It is rocky but has no mountains and is blessed with white sandy beaches. The coastline of Iona is dotted with white-painted cottages with a dense cluster of properties around its harbour with a small treeline behind them. In many ways, it could be mistaken for any one of the rural harbours around the coast of Scotland or the Hebrides but it is made uniquely distinctive and markedly Holy by the ancient cathedral just inland from its shoreline.

Those arriving by ferry could alight at the jetty (also referred to as the pier) at Baile Mòr. If arriving by steamer, the water near the jetty was not deep enough to accommodate the draft of a steamer, so it would drop anchor in the bay and passengers and their luggage would decant into smaller boats capable of carrying thirty to forty passengers at a time. These boats were all manned by experienced islander boatmen who would row visitors from the ship to the jetty where they would dock alongside and the passengers would alight onto the island. The steamer and landing was quite an adventure in itself.

There certainly is an atmosphere about Iona, something difficult to adequately encapsulate in words. Pilgrims make the journey to Iona to experience it as the centre of Celtic Christianity founded by St Columb in the sixth century, but even those who come as visitors who travel the ancient hallowed paths and visit its sacred sites speak of 'connecting' with sacred wisdom and leaving transformed and renewed for their journey ahead.

Visitors who are spiritual often describe Iona as a 'thin place' because it is believed to be one of those special places on this earth where the physical and spiritual worlds meet and even encounters with the Divine seem possible. But not all could cope with the intensity of their experiences. In the nineteenth century, a stone in the graveyard of the old nunnery was pointed out to visitors as the marker to one who had been obliged to leave holy orders. Henry Graham sent a sketch of it to his father, noting it as 'tombstone of the frail nun … though it is broken like her vows and cracked like her expectation, poor thing'.[2] As Mrs Alison Johnson of the St Columba hotel would candidly comment in far more recent times to Richard Wilson when he came to research his *Scotland's Unsolved Mysteries* book in the 1980s: 'Iona is a strong place. It can attract some 'interesting' types and, if people are a little unbalanced when they arrive here, it can overbalance them completely'.[3]

The Christian foundations on Iona date back to 563 AD when St Columba sailed away from Ireland in a coracle with twelve companions

---

2. Quoted in MacArthur, E. Mairi, *Columba's Island* (Edinburgh University Press, 1995)
3. Wilson, Richard, *Scotland's Unsolved Mysteries* (revised edition, Robert Hale, 1995)

and landed on Iona and started a Christian community there that spread across Scotland and beyond. Consequently, Iona is widely considered the cradle of Celtic Christianity but what should not be forgotten is that the church erected by Columba on the island was built on the scene of what would have been classed as a murder in the eyes of modern law.

When Columba landed on Iona, he was already considered a Holy man with miraculous happenings attributed to him from his time in Ireland. In one terrible incident, while he was at Leinster reading with a member of his brethren in a field, they witnessed the murder of a young woman committed by a tribesman in front of them. The monks had tried to reach her and intervene but they were too late. The brother with Columba turned to him and asked if God would let the horrific deed go unpunished? Columba replied that as soon as the soul of the girl ascended to heaven, the soul of the murderer would go down to hell. No sooner had he uttered those words, the tribesman fell down dead without a mark of violence upon him.

Once settled on Iona, Columba and his brethren began their missionary work, converting the Picts to Christianity not by crusade but by deeds and even miracles across Scotland, such as his banishment of a water beast from the River Ness (which has been suggested was the Loch Ness Monster) in 565 AD. Adomnán recorded how, on one occasion, Columba told his brethren he wished to travel alone to the western plain of Iona but one of his brothers followed him and watched from a nearby hill. From his vantage point, he saw Columba standing on a mound on the plain, praying with his hands spread out and, looking up toward heaven, then suddenly the brother saw:

> … many holy angels, clad in white garments, bright citizens of the Heavenly Country, flying to Columba with wonderful swiftness. They began to stand around him as he prayed. And after some conversation with the blessed man, that celestial band sped quickly back to heaven.

The hill where this event is believed to have taken place is known as Cnoc nan Aingeal – the hill of angels or hill of fires. Located just west of the centre of Iona, to the south of the road leading to the Machair and visible across the Machair from Dùn Bhuirg, it remains the largest of many knolls on the island. It is also a pre-Christian ancient sacred site, known as Sithean Mòr or Faery Mound. Within and around the mound, it has been long believed to be a habitual haunt of faery folk, as we have seen in the story of the two young men who had been fishing. People have been known to disappear there. It is also said the gentle strains of faery music are said to emanate from within, heard by islanders and visitors alike.

There are anecdotal stories of a stone circle; one standing on the site up to the eighteenth century when islanders ran horses sunwise around the mound on the feast day of St Michael. Iona historian E. Mairi MacArthur notes:

> … stories of fairy music and dancing abounded and on the great quarterly festival of May Day, Lâtha Bealltainn, fires were said to be kindled on its summit and the cattle driven through in an act of purification.[4]

As the seasons change, Gaelic folklore also holds that the *sidhe* move home and hold their gatherings of dancing and celebration. Some folks believed it was best to avoid being out on May Day night lest you get caught up in the 'flitting' but, as ever, the islanders seem to have had no qualms about mixing with the fae.

Alasdair Alpin MacGregor tells the salutary tale of a lady holidaying on Iona who expressed a desire to visit the Faery Mound at night:

> Disregarding the natives' warning that she might regret having done so, she set out for it alone. An hour or two later she returned greatly shaken. She resolutely declined to give an account of her experience.[5]

Another legend tells of how when Columba and his brethren attempted to build a church of stone, what they built by day would be reduced to ruins by the next morning. After this happened several times, Columba was supposedly informed by 'divine intimation' that the land required

---

4. MacArthur, E. Mairi, *Columba's Island* (Edinburgh University Press, 1995)
5. MacGregor, Alasdair Alpin, *The Ghost Book* (Hale, 1955)

a human sacrifice if the walls of the building were to remain standing. One of Columb's brethren named Oran (also recorded as Odran or in the Irish form of Odhrán) offered himself to be buried alive so his body would consecrate the land. Oran thus became the first Christian to be buried on Iona and he would be made a Saint.

In some versions of the story, it does not end there. Columba wanted to see Oran once more three days after his burial so he ordered that the grave be re-opened. In Fiona MacLeod's account of the tale:

Colum opened the grave, to look once more on the face of the dead brother, when to the amazed fear of the monks and the bitter anger of the abbot himself, Oran opened his eyes and exclaimed, 'There is no such great wonder in death, nor is Hell what it has been described.' At this, Colum straight-away cried: "Uir, ùir, air sùil Odhrain! mu'n labhair e tuille comhraidh" (Earth, earth on Oran's eyes, lest he further blab)[6]

The grave was hastily filled in again as instructed. Oran's words as the soil was shovelled back on top of him are not recorded.

Arguably, the death of Oran was a human blood sacrifice akin to pagan rites and magic. Early Christians absorbed many Anglo-Saxon pagan beliefs and even endowed the Christian God and Jesus with the attributes of pagan gods. Pagan symbolism, such as green men and woodwose, can often be found carved among the Christian decorations outside and within churches up to the medieval period and pagan rituals can be found as the basis for some elements of Christian rituals, especially burials, so it is not beyond possibility that even such a rite as the sacrifice of Oran could be carried out, especially if it had been suggested by 'divine intimation'. To other eyes, what Columba did could be viewed as murder.

The monastery St Columba became a centre of Celtic Christianity and sacred learning, which also became a spiritual land of kings and king-making. In his book *Iona: Its History and Antiquities* (1898), the Reverend Archibald Macmillan, Rector of Iona, records tradition saying Columba crowned Áedán King of the Scots as he sat upon 'the stone of destiny' in

---

6. MacLeod, Fiona (Sharp, William), *Iona* (Heinemann, 1910)

574 AD in a ceremony conducted on the island. Although only regarded as tradition when writing in the late seventh century, Adomnán also records that Áedán was ordained as king there by Columba.[7] According to those same traditions, the stone was removed to Dunstaffnage Castle near Oban for safekeeping. It was subsequently moved by King Kenneth MacAlpin in 841 AD to the religious house of the Culdees at Scone near Perth. The Culdees observed a primitive form of Christian worship without the pomp of Roman Christianity and had their chief seat on Iona, so it was not as if the stone was completely removed from the order of the Culdees. The stone would then reside in Scone Abbey when that was built in the twelfth century, hence it became known as 'The Stone of Scone'.

The Stone of Scone was captured by the forces of King Edward I of England in 1296 and was removed to Westminster Abbey in London, where it would be used in the coronation of English and British monarchs. Initially, the monarchs-to-be were crowned seated on the stone itself but a wooden platform for the stone enabled it to be incorporated into the Coronation Chair in the seventeenth century. The stone was returned to Scotland in 1996 and was initially kept at Edinburgh Castle among the Honours of Scotland. In 2024, the stone was removed to Perth Museum and a special display dedicated to it. The stone, however, remains the property of the Crown and is transported with due reverence to London and placed on the platform in the chair for coronations.

The church and subsequent monastery built on Columba's foundation on Iona became a religious house of considerable significance and contained a scriptorium where the Book of Kells may well have been written towards the end of the eighth century. The problem was Iona and its peaceful religious community fell easy prey to Viking raiders. It was sacked on a number of occasions. Infamously, 68 monks were slaughtered during a Viking raid in 806. The monks who survived the attack fled to the Abbey of Kells in Ireland, taking the magnificent illuminated book they had been working on with them. The monastery was finally abandoned in 849; very little of it remains today to give any indication any religious house ever stood on the site. Perhaps the blood sacrifice of a Christian at its foundation was not such a great idea after all.

---

7. Adomnán, III, 5, Byrne, Francis *Irish Kings and High Kings* (Batsford, 1973)

When the Kingdom of Scotland was established in the late ninth century, the ruling dynasty traced its origins to Iona and the Reilig Odhrán (St Oran's Chapel Cemetery) became the sacred place for the burial of many kings between the ninth and eleventh centuries. Donald Monro, Dean of the Isles' inventory of 1549, recorded 48 Scottish kings, eight Norwegian Kings and four Irish Kings buried there. Among them is King Duncan, the basis of King Duncan in Shakespeare's *Macbeth*. Even the island gets a mention when Rosse enquires, 'Where is Duncan's body?' and Macduff replies:

Carried to Colmekill [one of various old names for Iona],
The sacred storehouse of his predecessors,
And the guardian of his bones.

In that same burying ground was buried Macbeth (1005–1057), 'The Red King', who was immortalised in Shakespeare's play that bears his name.

The Benedictine Abbey was founded on Iona about the year 1203 and was dissolved at the time of the Reformation in the sixteenth century, the Abbey buildings went into decline, fell into ruin and were left open to the elements. Dr Samuel Johnson recorded his visit to Iona with his friend James Boswell in *A Journey to the Western Isles of Scotland* (1775). They found the religious houses that once stood proudly on the island in ruins. The chapel of the nunnery was used by the inhabitants as a cow-house and Johnson bemoaned how the floor was thus caused to be too miry for examination, adding:

The roof of this, as of all the other buildings, is totally destroyed, not only because timber quickly decays when it is neglected, but because in an island utterly destitute of wood, it was wanted for use, and was consequently, the first plunder of needy rapacity ... In one of the churches was a marble altar, which the superstition of the inhabitants has destroyed. Their opinion was, that a fragment of this stone was a defence against shipwrecks, fire, and miscarriages.[8]

---

8. Johnson, Dr Samuel, *A Journey to the Western Isles of Scotland* (Strahan and Cadell, 1775)

Johnson found the floor of the abbey ruins 'so incumbered with mud and rubbish, that we could make no discoveries of curious inscriptions'. He did, however, add an intriguing comment:

The place is said to be known where the black stones lie concealed, on which the old Highland Chiefs, when they made contracts and alliances, used to take the oath, which was considered as more sacred than any other obligation, and which could not be violated without the blackest infamy.[9]

Purely as an aside, but as a lover of mysteries, I find it intriguing to note this when considering the debate over the Stone of Destiny, later known as The Stone of Scone being *the* true Stone of Destiny. Although undoubtedly of quite some antiquity, the earliest descriptions of the sacred stone upon which Áedán sat to be crowned King of the Scots by St Columba on Iona in 574 AD describe it as a black stone with a concave shape like a round chair. The stone currently believed to be the Stone of Destiny simply does not look like that. Perhaps the true stone never left Iona after all and remains hidden, waiting to be rediscovered.

In parting from Iona, Dr Johnson remarked:

The inhabitants are remarkably gross, and remarkably neglected: I know not if they are visited by any Minister. The Island, which was once the metropolis of learning and piety, has now no school for education, nor temple for worship, only two inhabitants that can speak English, and not one that can write or read.[10]

Gaelic would remain spoken on Iona well into the twentieth century but they would not remain without a house of worship nor a minister to tend to his flock for quite so long. A modest parish church was built in 1828 to designs by engineer Thomas Telford by The Church of Scotland and a school would follow soon afterwards. By the twentieth century, the residents of Iona were firmly Presbyterian and the faith demanded the veneration of saints was renounced, even on the island synonymous with

9. Johnson, Dr Samuel, *A Journey to the Western Isles of Scotland* (Strahan and Cadell, 1775)
10. Johnson, Dr Samuel, *A Journey to the Western Isles of Scotland* (Strahan and Cadell, 1775)

St Columba. Islanders were also acutely suspicious of other denominations, particularly Roman Catholics and the Episcopalians.

Iona may have appeared to have had no organised worship for many years afterwards. Some outsiders would say they became 'Godless' but it was not that clear cut. The parish of Kilfinichen and Kilvikeon on Mull included the inhabited islands of Iona, Earraid, and Inchkenneth in its parish and the minister although resident on Mull would deliver sermons on Iona four times a year and minister to his flock for christenings, marriages and funeral as required. Consequently, a primitive form of Christianity, unregulated by any formal church, had evolved on Iona and had become entwined in superstition, charms for various purposes and folk medicine.

For example, the incantation to repel the evil eye was:

> It is mine own eye
> It is the eye of God,
> It is the eye of God's Son
> Which shall repel this,
> Which shall combat this…
>
> On the little fairy women
> Who are reeling in the knoll,
> Who are biding in the heath,
> Who are filling the cavities

and, as in *The Charm of the Threads*:

> I place the protection of God about thee,
> Blind folk over thee;
> Mayest thou be shielded from every peril;
> May the Gospel of the God of grace
> Be from thy crown to the ground about thee.
> May men love thee
> And women not work thee harm.

These are but two recorded examples of many. You will also notice the recurrent theme of protection from women, both fae and corporeal, within the verses.

As Francis Thompson pointed out in *The Supernatural Highlands*:

It [witchcraft] was also associated with rural poverty in areas normally inaccessible and remote from centre of population, areas which were breeding grounds for variations of orthodox religious beliefs. These areas in fact have often been proved to have a greater resistance to the introduction of new orthodoxies and again and again have to be won back to sound religion…the Highlands relapsed into 'paganism' and required rescue operations to be mounted by the new Puritan movement of the eighteenth century. Gospel carried into the unfeudal, half-Christian societies of remote parts inevitably, in that different world, found that its success was always transitory: that the ancient habits of thought and practice always reasserted themselves.

Iona was so small and its Christianity so entwined in folklore that the islanders would ensure anyone found transgressing the norms of their religion would have been swiftly and robustly dealt with. Historically, such places simply took matters into their own hands, such as at Forres in Moray, where in the sixteenth century, women accused of witchcraft were placed in stout barrels through which spikes were driven, then kicked down Cluny Hill and burned where the barrels stopped.

There was also the incident at Pittenweem in January 1705 that was the denouement of a season of witch persecution in the East Neuk of Fife. Janet Cornfoot had been accused of witchcraft and had escaped her captors. When she was recaptured, she was dragged by her heels to the seafront, was then beaten and strung up on a rope between the ship and the shore, and stoned. She was then taken down and placed under a door upon which stones were piled on top by villagers until she was crushed to death. And then a local man drove his horse and cart over the door several times to make sure she was dead. There were no reprisals from authorities for either incident. In fact, through both judicial process and locals taking action, it is estimated over 2,500 individuals, mostly women, were executed for witchcraft in Scotland between 1563 and 1727.

These cases are extremes but faith and passion run deep and old ways die hardest in remote areas.

So, dare it be mentioned that in a ritual held each year on the Thursday before Easter on Iona, the sea was supplicated by being given a quantity of brochan (porridge made with oatmeal) poured from a great pot from each headland? Or that Marie was present on the island in November, known as *Blōtmōnaþ*, the month that roughly corresponds with November recorded by the Anglo-Saxon chronicler, The Venerable Bede in *De temporum ratione* (The Reckoning of Time) (725 AD) as the month 'when our forefathers were heathens' in which living flesh sacrifices (usually cattle) were made to their chosen Gods.

The Presbyterian faith was accepted and its regulations followed on Iona, but any minister taking up residence on the island would rapidly be left under no illusions that the acceptance of him and his church would be on the terms of the islanders. The island of Iona remained slow to embrace the trappings of the modern world as a whole. Walking and horse-drawn transport were the order of the day. Motor vehicles were a rare sight on Iona and the roads on the island far from suitable for them. Life was simple and that was the way they liked it.

In the 1920s, a regular visitor to Iona wrote warmly of its local characters and colour and how calling in at the post office 'for a crack' with Angus MacPhail, the postmaster, or to blether with others waiting for the mail was 'one of the island's most modern entertainments'.[11] The first wireless radio was bought by the Cameron family of Traighmòr in 1923 and such was the island that when Angus MacPhail died in November 1931 after 35 years as the Iona postmaster, he could proudly say he had been instrumental in the introduction of the telegraph system to the island but it was much to his regret the first telephone was still to be installed on Iona.[12]

Despite the Presbyterian observances, islanders remained superstitious and even clung to beliefs in old Gods for luck and in folk medicine. Sunday was to be strictly observed as a sacred day when no work, chore or labour was permitted; not even the ferry would run. The necessity to observe sacred Sundays was reinforced by a salutary folktale that was told

---

11. MacArthur, E. Mairi, *Columba's Island* (Edinburgh University Press, 1995)
12. *Oban Times*, 5 December 1931

in a variety of forms on the islands of the inner Hebrides. A version of the story was published in the *Oban Times* in 1911:

> A young girl 'thrang' with work, and anxious to begin early on Monday morning, some dying operations, proposed to go out on Sunday to gather the necessary plants, and make them ready against the next day. Her mother sternly forbade her to go, but she would not be withheld and started on her way. Her mother, horrified beyond measure, lost control of herself and solemnly cursed her daughter, saying 'Go forth; nor return here.' Nothing more was ever heard of her. Her creel and hook were found, and round the place where they were discovered were signs of combat. Only from henceforth has been seen a wandering light as he trudges home over the moorland path. The light jumps three times and seen closely enough resembles lights with a light within.[13]

The article published under the title of *Supernatural Lights* also mentions how watchers by death beds 'are made aware of greenish lights, dim and nebulous, floating in the air in the room. On Iona the strange lights seen to float over the area where a sudden or violent death has taken place are blue. The article continues:

> Strange lights, sometimes called Will O' The Wisp, Jack o' Lantern and Sprinkie are common. Around them have grown up many tales and superstitions. In the island of Tiree that are known as fairy lights (Teine Sith) are often seen in churchyards or on boggy ground. Such ground is only too common in the Highlands, and therefore many of the stories of mysterious lights are cradled there. In many cases these lights are associated with death. Before any violent death, from whatever cause (though it is chiefly suicides), a light is seen hovering over the spot where it is to take place.[14]

Marie Fornario was also drawn to the island of Iona again soon after her first visit because it was a place that could offer her peace and quiet

---

13. *Oban Times*, 28 October 1911
14. *Oban Times*, 28 October 1911

for her contemplations and writing. She would undoubtedly have been influenced by the eulogic writing of the author Fiona MacLeod, whose works she adored, notably, *Iona* (1910), in which MacLeod explained:

> There is one Iona, a little island of the west. There is another Iona, of which I would speak. I do not say that it lies open to all. It is as we come that we find. If we come, bringing nothing with us, we go away ill-content, having seen and heard nothing of what we had vaguely expected to see or hear. It is another Iona than to Iona of sacred memories and prophesies: Iona the metropolis of dreams. None can understand it who does not see it through its pagan light, its Christian light, its singular blending of paganism and romance and spiritual beauty. There is, too, an Iona that is more than Gaelic, that is more than a place rainbow-lot with the seven desires of the world, the Iona that, if we will it so, is a mirror of your heart and mine.[15]

Iona would also be somewhere if she believed the stories of her friend Lucy Bruce (and it is highly likely that she did), where Marie would have the chance to commune with her beloved *Sidhe*. I have met several people over the years who have told me candidly that they firmly believe in aliens from other planets or dimensions; their belief extends to aliens abducting humans from the earth and say they are mentally prepared and wish the aliens would take them. Perhaps Marie had hoped to cross over into the faery world on Iona in a similar way.

She was no doubt aware of the dangers of this course of action. Crossing to the world of the Faery folk could have fatal consequences, as demonstrated in *The Immortal Hour*, nor would people on Iona be unduly worried by such an occurrence. As late as the 1970s, Francis Thompson would write in *The Supernatural Highlands*: 'Of all the characters and beings in the supernatural world of the Highlander, the fairy stands closest to him'.[16] In the book, *Iona*, Fiona MacLeod (real name William Sharp) tells the tale of when he was travelling to Tiree on an unspecified date, but it would have been in the latter half of the nineteenth century, when he stopped off at Iona to call upon an elderly woman named Giorsal.

---

15. MacLeod, Fiona, (Sharp, William), *Iona* (Heinemann, 1910)
16. Thompson, France, *The Supernatural Highlands* (Robert Hale, 1976)

She was not island-born but Scottish by birth, yet islanders still called her a foreigner.

Giorsal had a daughter named Ealàsaidh or, in English, she was Elsie. After being welcomed into the cottage, Sharp enquired about Elsie. The mother did not seem unperturbed and simply said, 'She is gone', and carried on pottering around her kitchen. On Sharp querying 'Gone', Giorsal explained, 'She's gone. That's all I know.' She had not found a love and left the island, nor had she been found dead or drowned nor had she been the victim of some tragic accident or sudden illness. Elsie had, however, been troubled by recurrent dreams of a ghostly black-robed monk, one of those known on the island as the Culdees:

She [Elsie] said she wished Siól Leoid [The Clan MacLeod] had come to Iona before Colum built the big church. And for why? Well, there's this, for one thing: for months a monk had come to her o' nights in her sleep, an'said he would kill her, because she was a heathen.[17]

Elsie went to see a local priest but he dismissed her as just being foolish and became angry with her for wasting his time. So she went to see a local wise woman:

Mary Gillespie out by the lochan beyond Fionnaphort on the Ross yonder – her that has the sight an' a power o' the old wisdom. After that she took to meeting friends in the moonshine.[18]

The monk, however, came again and to her to go over to them and threatened if she failed to comply, they would kill her. Elsie was told by her friends in the moonlight that up between Sgéur Iolaire and Cnoc Druidean, there was a path where no monk could go. It was where the monks burneda human woman who they thought was a witch who was spreading deadly plague. Turned out she was one of the Sorrows of the Shee (Elvin people).

---

17. MacLeod, Fiona, (Sharp, William), *Iona* (Heinemann, 1910)
18. MacLeod, Fiona, (Sharp, William), *Iona* (Heinemann, 1910)

On the January night before she disappeared, Elsie had come into the cottage bearing wild roses. Her mother exclaimed, 'Breisleach! What's the meanin' o' roses in January.' The girl just looked at her and appeared frightened, threw the roses on the fire and left the following day. A heavy gale was tearing through the sound when she just went off. Her mother recalled:

> She just went out o' the house again cryin.' I asked her what was wrong wi' her. She turned and smiled, and because of that terrifying smile I couldna' say a word. She went up behind the Ruins, an' no one saw her after that but Ian Donn. He saw her among the bulrushes in the swamp over by Staonaig. She was laughing and talking to the reeds, or to the wind in the reeds…[19]

Alasdair Alpin MacGregor would remark, 'They say in Iona that the south end of the island [where Staonaig Hill is located] has something uncanny about it. Lucy Bruce talks to the elementals there: Johnnie MacMillan smells death there'.[20] I am convinced it was far from by chance that Marie Fornario's dead body was found on Staonaig Hill in 1929.

Young Elsie was not the only person to disappear from that small island under mysterious circumstances in the later nineteenth century. Alasdair Alpin MacGregor relates a story of a friend's father who lived on Iona all his life who when a boy had been returning from a fishing trip from the west side of the island where he had been fishing with a friend when they passed the Faery Mound (Sithean Mòr) and his pal who was carrying their day's catch sat down for a moment to rest – and disappeared! Now Iona is a small island. His parents, fraught with worry, organised a search for the lad but there was no sign of him and there really was nowhere the boy would have been hidden on the island without anyone knowing. The boy turned up a year later on the same spot. Dazed and unable to account for where he had been. The fish he had caught a year before were still in his hand and were still as fresh as the day he had caught them.[21]

---

19. MacLeod, Fiona, (Sharp, William), *Iona* (Heinemann, 1910)
20. MacGregor, Alasdair Alpin, *The Ghost Book* (Robert Hale, 1955)
21. MacGregor, Alasdair Alpin, *The Ghost Book* (Robert Hale, 1955)

In another version of the story recorded by Reverend John Gregorson Campbell in *Superstitions of the Highlands and Islands of Scotland* (Glasgow 1900), more likely a retelling of the same story because it is too similar to relate to a different incident, the two friends who had been fishing saw a door open in the Faery Mound and went inside.

One of them joined the dancers, without waiting to lay down the string of fish he had in his hand. The other stuck a fish-hook in the door and when he wished made his escape. He came back for his companion that day twelvemonths, and found him still dancing with the string of fish in his hand. On taking him to the open air the fish dropped from the string, rotten.[22]

Paranormal occurrences such as sudden deaths and even disappearances seem to be perceived as nothing particularly disturbing on Iona and Mull. Less than five years before Marie arrived on Iona, the *Oban Times* reported the disappearance of Ellen Beaton (21) from neighbouring Mull in March 1925. Ellen was a student in teacher training at Moray House Training College in Edinburgh. Ellen was staying with her sister while she studied there and she left a note for her on 27 February stating she was going to visit their parents at Tobermory. She was not seen again. The newspaper report concluded by mentioning her brother '…had disappeared from their house in Tobermory over four years ago without anything being heard of him beyond an unconfirmed rumour that he had gone to America'.[23] The press conveyed no overdue concern nor any efforts undertaken by local people or the police to find these two missing people nor is there a follow up story of either being found again.

There are also bizarre explanations of why people disappear published in Scottish and even national newspapers of the day, such as the discovery of the charred remains of a child's body on Mither Tap, the highest mountain of the Bennachie group in Aberdeenshire in March 1921. Local authorities announced the discovery of the remains was 'a partial solution' to the disappearance of Frances Stephen Hay (2) from his

---

22. Campbell, Reverend John Gregorson, *Superstitions of the Highlands and Islands of Scotland* (Glasgow, 1900)
23. *Oban Times*, 14 March 1925

home at Dorlethen Farm, Pitcable, seven years earlier on the afternoon of Sunday, 10 May 1914.

A search conducted by police officers and over 400 volunteers at the time of the boy's disappearance covered a thirty-mile radius but drew a blank. The body believed to be that of the missing child found in 1921 was discovered some two miles from the cottage from where he had disappeared. Apparently, the area had previously been covered in undergrowth that had been swept by fire the previous year, hence the burning to the body. The child being found so far from where it went missing, it was considered impossible for the little one to have crawled up the steep hillside covered in undergrowth to where it had been found, so the conclusion was drawn that the infant must have been 'carried away by an eagle'.[24]

---

24. *Dundee Evening Telegraph*, 22 March 1921

Chapter 9

Dance with the Devil in the Pale Moonlight

Eochaidh: *My dreams! My dreams! Give me my dream!*
Dalua: *There is none left but this … the dream of death*
Fiona MacLeod

In the late summer of 1929, Marie Fornario informed her housekeeper, Mrs Varney, that she intended to go to Scotland to contemplate a book she intended to write. As time went on, it became clear that Marie had made up her mind that she would go to Iona where she planned to spend the winter and packed accordingly. As she departed in late August, she told Mrs Varney: 'I am going out to the far beyond, but I shall return.' Mrs Varney knew full well her employer knew she would understand when she said 'far beyond' that she did not just mean a distance in miles. She would not only be away in the Highlands but also the 'far beyond' was the world she would be visiting psychically.

Despite having told her housekeeper she would be travelling alone, when Marie arrived on Iona on a fine, sunny day with several locals around her, her appearance in her colourful hand-woven clothes, refined bearing and long dark hair certainly made her stand out. On a small island where some of the simplest matters, from the latest arrival of mail or visitors, can be and often are the topic of conversation, Marie was noticed. It would also be recalled that she was accompanied by another woman and they stayed with a Mrs Campbell in the smattering of houses that make up the village of Baile Mor (a somewhat ironic name which translates as 'Big Town') that constitutes the most significant settlement on the island. The women were seen going into one of the short rows of terraced or detached cottages that face the jetty where the ferry lands.

Marie appeared to be on friendly terms with the woman she arrived with but it is unclear if they had just met and struck up a friendship as fellow pilgrims on their way to Iona or if they had been established friends who had arranged to travel together. It is possible, in the absence of stronger candidates, that if she had met up with a friend, it would have been either Iona McDonald or Lucy Bruce (later Mrs Iona Cammell), the friends she had made through writing for *The Occult Review*, who both knew and loved Iona and had stayed there on several previous occasions and I am sure either of them would have leapt at the chance to meet up with a friend and show them the island. The unidentified friend then departed a few days later, leaving Marie to enjoy Iona in peace and so she could get on with her contemplations and writing.

When her friend left, Marie went to stay at Traighmòr (pronounced 'try vohr'). Located about a half a mile south-west and a ten-minute walk from the village, this more remote croft is a simple two-storey grey, stone-built cottage with four dormer windows that is charmingly situated only a stone's throw from the Traigh Mhor (Big Beach) with its white sand from which the croft takes its name. The croft was the home of Donald Cameron (1862–1946), his wife Catherine, known as 'Kitty' (1879–1960) and their three children: Catherine, known as 'Katie' (born 1908), Mary known as 'Molly' (born 1910), and Calum (born 1916).

Adverts placed in *The Scotsman* offering the croft of Traighmòr as a place to stay in 1929 describe it as a Board residence in an ideal situation for bathing, boating and golf.[1] Marie would have loved it for the solitude, peace and quiet that it offered and for the kind owners who provided a warm welcome and board but left her to be without being intrusive. The Camerons' early impressions of Marie were recorded by Alasdair Alpin MacGregor:

When she arrived she was in anything but robust health. The little exercise she seemed able to take amounted to no more than a daily walk of a few hundred yards along the sandy beach, at no great distance from the Camerons'. Sometimes, owing to fatigue, she did not leave her room for days.[2]

Iona McDonald described Marie as being 'of a frank and friendly disposition', and she soon made friends with her hosts and islanders. The

---

1. *The Scotsman*, 14 August 1929
2. MacGregor, Alasdair Alpin, *The Ghost Book* (Robert Hale, 1955)

Camerons were naturally intrigued by their guest. Mrs Kitty Cameron wondered why their guest would exchange the gaiety of London for Iona, so she asked in conversation. Marie gladly answered with the reply that she had 'heard the call of the island' that offered the peace and tranquillity for which she yearned. The Camerons and other locals also noticed:

> From the day she landed on the island, she interested herself in its folklore, and became increasingly absorbed in the eerie and uncanny aspects of her Hebridean environment.[3]

As time went on, however, the Camerons became concerned as an air of mystery gathered about the woman they had staying upstairs 'in the attic' of their home when, as Alpin MacGregor explains:

> They discovered, or believed they discovered that their guest was given to secret and mystical practices. Exactly what they were, nobody could quite say. I am told she was a Rosicrucian. If it was as much as whispered the word among the Presbyterians of Columba's Isle, it would have been sufficient to confirm their suspicions of dangerous heterodoxy, suspicions already established whenever it became known that she never retired for the night without two little oil lamps glowing dimly in her room, and a glass of orange juice on her bedside table. When, however, she began to speak of visions she had seen in the heavens, and of messages received from the spirit world, they were quite horrified then, that faraway look they had seen in her eyes now denoted either madness or something diabolical.[4]

The Cameron's native predisposition toward anything of a supernatural character, however, tempered their attitude towards their guest. Mrs Cameron seems to have been the most inquisitive and amiable host, so she spoke with her often. She happened to notice Marie's silver jewellery had become black and tarnished and asked her about it. Marie simply replied that it always happened when she wore it. This is curious because solid sterling silver necklaces and rings don't tend to tarnish if they are

3. MacGregor, Alasdair Alpin, *The Ghost Book* (Robert Hale, 1955)
4. MacGregor, Alasdair Alpin, *The Ghost Book* (Robert Hale, 1955)

regularly worn or handled. They should only dull over long-term wear. However, chemicals from the body like sweat, alcohol or exposure to sulphur, such as that which can be emitted from decomposing seaweed, can tarnish silver or even turn it black more quickly.

Marie had taken to being out all day. Columba's Bay was clearly one of her favoured places and she was often seen there, seated on one of the mounds, engrossed in writing in one of her bound notebooks, so there is a possibility it was the sea air and seaweed that were turning her jewellery black.

As time passed, however, the Camerons concerns over Marie continued to mount:

> The strange lady with the strange look in her eyes and the strange ways seemed to be getting stranger. Mrs Cameron became positively alarmed when she mentioned that, if she went into a trance, she might remain in it for a week or more, and that, in such an event, nothing in the nature of medical aid was to be summoned. She must be left undisturbed.[5]

One day, when Marie had not returned at nightfall, the Camerons became anxious and began to organise a search party to see if she could be found in case she had suffered an accident. Marie turned up as they were about to set out. Apparently unphased by the worry she had caused, Marie explained that she had been so long because she had been sending telepathic messages.

According to MacGregor, as Marie learned more about the islands, she became fascinated by what was said to be the site of a pre-Christian settlement where the spirits of the dead were said to roam. He does not name the site but writes of how there was no road or track to get there. It was only accessible on foot over 'steep rocks and treacherous marshes'. Perhaps she had heard the stories of Staonnaig, located about a mile away from Traighmòr in the south of the island; the common ground where, in past times, the crofters of the east and the west of Iona came alternately to graze their cattle for fourteen days over the summer months. It was

---

5. MacGregor, Alasdair Alpin, *The Ghost Book* (Robert Hale, 1955)

there that Reverend John Gregorson Campbell, Minister of Tiree, records in *Superstitions of the Highlands and Islands of Scotland* (1900):

> In those days a Glaistig stayed in a hole of the rocks in Staonnaig, and the people, when at the summer pastures (diridh) poured milk every night in a stone for her.[6]

The Glaistig was a legendary creature often confused with the Banshi (also spelt Banshee). The major difference being the Glaistig was once a human woman who had been put under enchantments and to whom a 'fairy nature has been given' whereas the Banshi was a born and bred fairy woman who was never human. The Glaistig was particularly associated with being a protector or guardian of ancient ruins and the enclosures of livestock, especially cattle, rather than a harbinger of death. What both Glaistig and Banshi do have in common is they can both wail, as the Reverend Campbell went on to explain:

> The Glaistig was a tutelary being in the shape of a thin grey (tana glas) little woman, with long yellow hair reaching to her heels, dressed in green, haunting certain sites or farms, and watching in some cases over the house, in others over the cattle. She is called 'the Green Glaistig' (a Ghlaistig uaine) from her wan looks and dress of green, the characteristic Fairy colour. She is said to have been at first a woman of honourable position, a former mistress of the house, who had been put under enchantments and now had a Fairy nature given her … She was solitary in her habits, not more than one, unless when accompanied by her own young one, being found in the same haunt. Her strength was very great, much greater than that of any Fairy, and one yell of hers was sufficient to waken the echoes of distant hills. Strong men were said to have mastered her, but ordinarily people were afraid of meeting her. She might do them a mischief and leave them a token, by which they would have cause to remember the encounter.[7]

---

6. Campbell, Reverend John Gregorson, *Superstitions of the Highlands and Islands of Scotland* (Glasgow, 1900)

7. Campbell, Reverend John Gregorson, *Superstitions of the Highlands and Islands of Scotland* (Glasgow, 1900)

Marie had taken to going out on evening walks, but on one occasion, she did not return to Traighmòr until the following morning. She said she had lost her way and had to spend what she declared was 'a perfect night' on the moor. Although Marie did not say so directly, the Camerons concluded from one or two casual remarks she made later, she had been searching for the ancient haunted site in the dark. The question remains of if when she had her 'perfect night', had she found her perfect place under the stars and was performing a rite of healing and purification? Then perhaps at last she saw the 'Green Ray' at dawn. As the days passed, Marie went out more and more in the moonlight. She told the Camerons that she was studying the stars but when she came in, she would draw strange circles on pieces of paper. If she did not go out in the evening, she wrote by the light of her two oil lamps through the night and would be so exhausted by dawn she would go to bed for the rest of the day.

As each week passed, the Camerons and locals who had come to know Marie noticed marked changes in her as she became increasingly dishevelled and appeared somehow 'haunted':

Her face now showed nothing of the repose the islanders had noted when she first arrived in their midst. That expression had given way to one of dire distress; and she now spoke hurriedly, if not a little incoherently.[8]

Mrs Varney received a letter from Marie that had arrived around Saturday, 16 November, stating: 'Do not be surprised if you do not hear from me for a long time. I have a terrible healing case'.[9] Although generally a small eater, Marie had also developed a craving for double portions at mealtimes. These second helpings, she explained, were intended to benefit sick friends she was healing by telepathy.[10] She would also never close her curtains because she said she saw the faces of her previous patients in the clouds.

On Sunday, 17 November 1929, Marie rose unusually early in quite some panic and insisted to the Camerons that having received a message

---

8. MacGregor, Alasdair Alpin, *The Ghost Book* (Robert Hale, 1955)
9. *Reynolds's Newspaper*, 1 December 1929
10. *Daily Record*, 26 November 1929

Girls dressed as fairies ready to dance for a flower festival pageant, *c.* 1910

Frances Griffiths (9) photographed by her cousin Elsie Wright (16) with some of the dancing fairies at Cottingley Beck, Bradford, West Yorkshire, July 1917.

The Sphinx and pyramids on the Giza Plateau, Egypt, around the time of the birth of Marie Fornario in nearby Cairo, in 1896.

The leafy and sedate Leigham Court Road, Streatham, where Marie Fornario grew up with her grandparents at Leigham Holme, *c.* 1904.

An early twentieth-century theatrical reconstruction of a séance.

Sir Arthur Conan Doyle, notable advocate of spiritualism, communication with the dead, the photography of ghosts and fairies in the 1920s.

An elderly couple posing with a 'spirit' that was unseen at the time the photograph was taken but 'appeared' on the negative and print when they were developed.

Marthe Beraud (aka Eva C), a materialisation medium who appeared to be capable of amazing feats of mind power in the early twentieth century.

American magician Howard Thurston, who entertained audiences by apparently conjuring demons and spirits of the dead, live on stage.

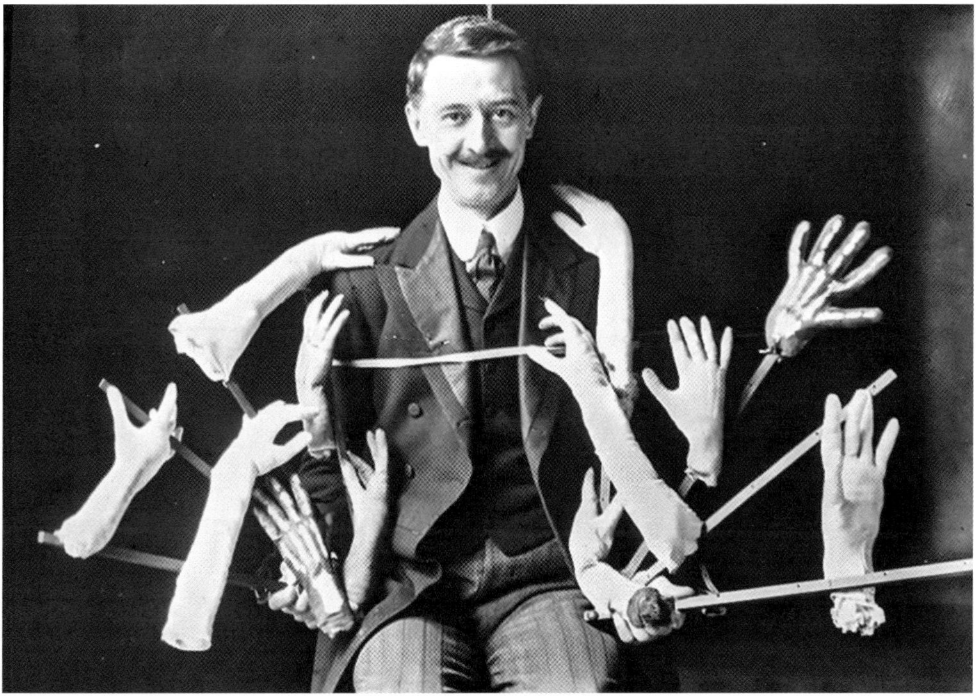

William Marriott, a British stage magician, who became well known for exposing fraudulent spiritualist mediums by publicly revealing the tricks of their trade.

Marie Fornario (right) and a fellow performer ready to play their roles at a historical pageant, *c.* 1914.

Violet Firth (Dion Fortune) in her radiant vestments.

Dust wrapper of the first edition of Dion Fortune's *The Secrets of Dr Taverner*, published by Noel Douglas (1926).

Illustration from *The Projection of the Astral Body* by Sylvan J. Muldoon and Hereward Carrington, published by Rider and Co in 1929.

King's Lynn Market Place, Norfolk, with The Duke's Head Hotel in the background as it would have looked when Theodore Moriarty dropped dead there on 18 August 1923.

Gwen Ffrangcon-Davies photographed in her role as Etain in *The Immortal Hour*, *c.* 1923.

Illustration by Meauille from the 1907 edition of Jules Verne's *Le Rayon-Vert* (The Green Ray).

AN ISLAND
TRAGEDY

Miss Norah Fornario, of Kew, said to be psychic, who was found dead, probably from exposure, on the lonely Isle of Iona.

The mysterious death of Miss Norah Fornario made the cover of the *Daily Mirror* on 28 November 1929.

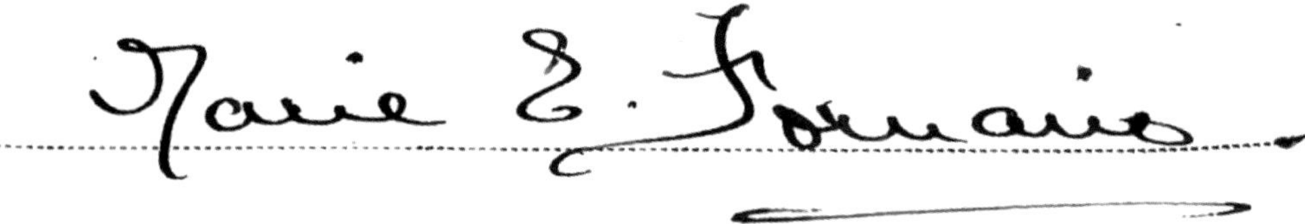

The formal signature of Marie E. Fornario on a legal document.

George Street and harbour, Oban, Argyllshire, Scotland in the 1920s. A steamer to Iona would leave from the North Pier here every day except Sunday.

The view from the hills around Oban, over the town and across the harbour to the Sound of Mull in the 1920s.

The cottages of the village of Baile Mòr with the Abbey in the background, the first view many visitors have after they land at the harbour on Iona, *c.* 1900.

The Street, Baile Mòr, Iona in the 1920s.

Iona Abbey and the ruins of St Oran's Chapel, *c.* 1929. Marie Fornario was buried in the adjoining Reilig Odhrán (St Oran's Chapel Cemetery).

The jetty (also referred to as the pier) at Baile Mòr with visitors and locals awaiting the arrival of a steamer, *c.* 1929.

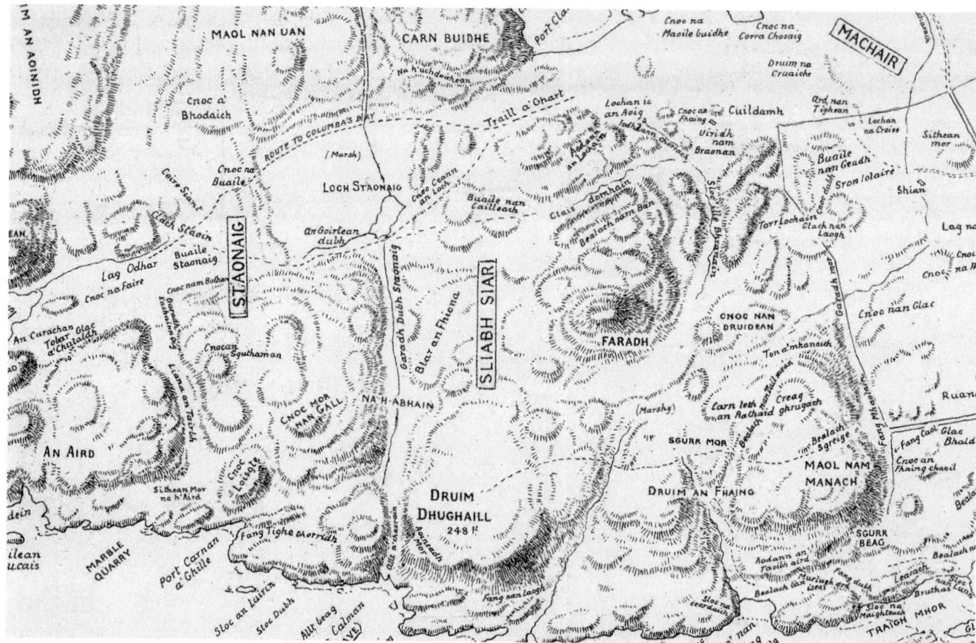

Section a of Map of Iona, *c.* 1929. Traigh Mhor is bottom right, Staonaig Hill, where Marie Fornario was found dead, is centre left.

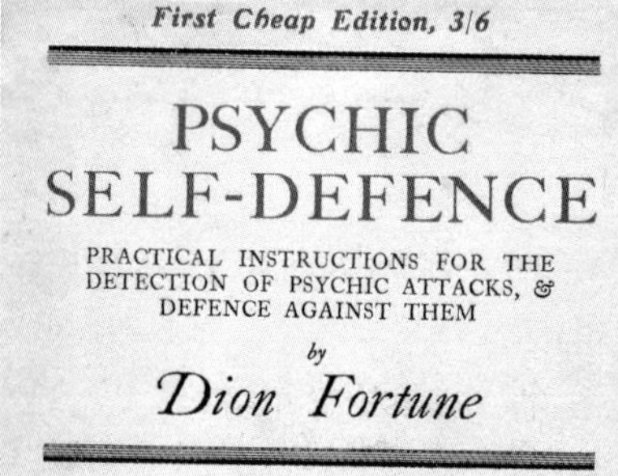

Cover 'First Cheap Edition' of Dion Fortune's *Psychic Self Defence*. The hardback first edition of 1930 was the first book to mention 'The recent tragedy in Iona'.

Aleister Crowley (1875–1947) wearing A∴A∴ Adeptus Major robes with the hood folded into a hat, *c.* 1909.

Florence Farr (1860–1917), actress, Golden Dawn member and author of the books *Egyptian Magic* and *The Dancing Faun*.

W B Yeats (1865–1939), poet and long-serving member of the Golden Dawn.

Leila Waddell (1880–1932) with her violin wearing a full A∴A∴ Dominus Liminis robe with the hood folded and worn as a hat, photographed in 1910.

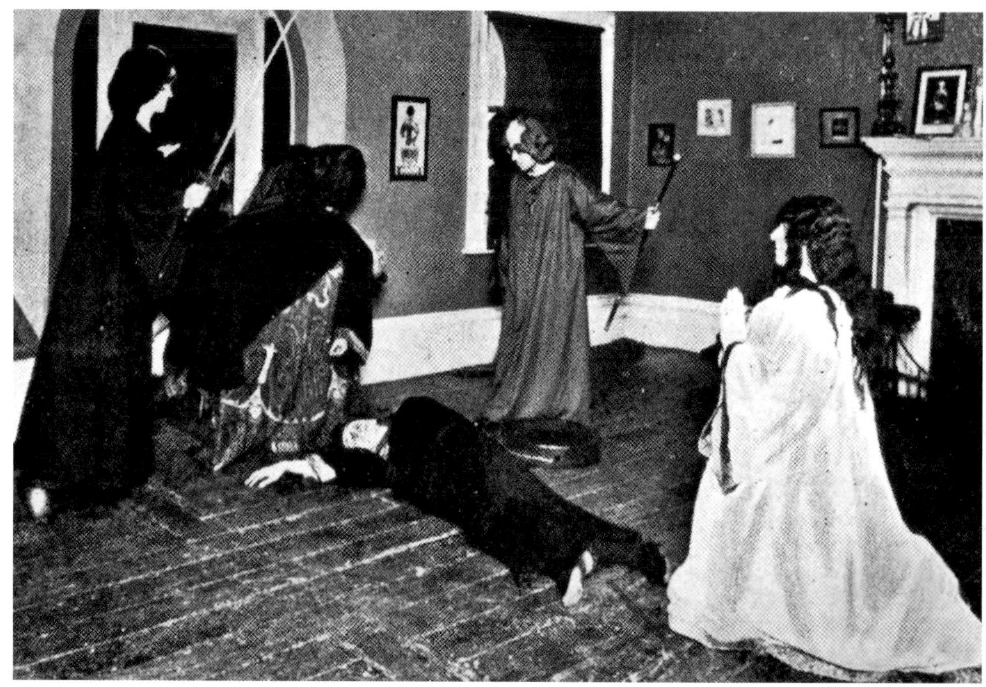

The Rite of Saturn, 'suicide of the Atheist', being performed at Crowley's studio flat at 124 Victoria Street, London S.W., 1910.

The hypnotic stare of Aleister Crowley, *c.* 1930.

American actress Jane Wolfe (1875–1958), one of Crowley's acolytes at the Abbey of Thelema at Cefalù, Sicily.

Singer, dancer and West End model 'Tiger Woman' Betty May (1894–1980).

Artist and sculptor, Nina Hamnett, painted by Roger Eliot Fry (1917).

Maria Teresa Sanchez and Aleister Crowley, *c.* 1929.

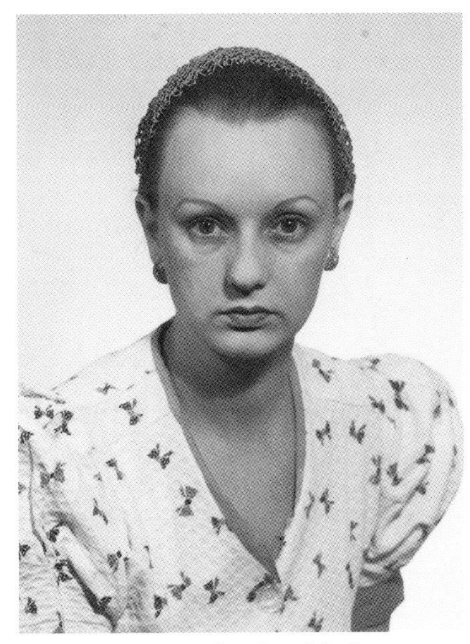

Surrealist artist and author, Ithell Colquhoun (1906–1988).

Aleister Crowley, *c.* 1936.

Cover of one of the 'last ritual' booklets with artwork by Lady Frieda Harris distributed to those who attended Aleister Crowley's cremation on 5 December 1947.

Boleskine Burial Ground, between the banks of Loch Ness and Boleskine House, once home and ritual centre for Aleister Crowley. More than history lingers here …

she had to pack and leave the island at once. It should be remembered this was a Sunday, everywhere was closed and no one could recall her receiving a letter or telegram the previous day, so it must be assumed the message had come to her telepathically. Even when it was pointed out to Marie that no ferry services ran from Iona on a Sunday, she remained resolute that she must go at all costs. Uncomfortable at engaging in any labours on a Sunday, the Camerons still helped Marie to pack and by late afternoon, all her belongings were packed and ready to be transported to the jetty and Marie went to her room to rest.

In the evening, however, Marie opened her door and told Mrs Cameron that her dire need to depart no longer appeared necessary and the Camerons helped her unpack. As they did so, they noticed a change in Marie's face, which had become 'weirdly pallid' and it was with resignation rather than relief after coming through such a traumatic time that she appeared to have somehow aged over those frantic hours of packing. Marie had calmed down and spent the early evening chatting 'pleasantly and rationally' with the Camerons and then retired to bed around 9.00 pm.[11] When interviewed by Richard Wilson for his *Scotland's Unsolved Murders* book in the 1980s, the Camerons' son Calum, aged 12 in 1929, looked back on that evening and recalled, 'Aye, she was a' right on the Sunday night.'[12]

On the Monday morning of 18 November, when Calum's elder sister Molly took Miss Fornario's breakfast up and knocked on her door, she received no reply. Molly could smell burning so she entered the room, only to find it empty. There was no disorder and no signs to indicate Marie had left in any haste. The bedclothes were turned down from the pillows, the oil lamps whose light she used to write through the night were still alight, all her clothes appeared to be there and her items of jewellery, watch and hairpins were all placed in orderly fashion on the dressing table. The only thing that was out of the ordinary was the grate in the fireplace was filled with black remnants of what had once been pages of Marie's writing … but there was no sign of Marie.

No one in Traighmòr had heard her leave but the Camerons knew she often went on her wanderings at night and thought that was exactly what

11. MacGregor, Alasdair Alpin, *The Ghost Book* (Robert Hale, 1955)
12. Wilson, Richard, *Scotland's Unsolved Mysteries* (revised edition) (Hale, 1995)

she had done. As more time passed and when there was still no sign of their guest, the Camerons became more and more concerned. When Marie did not return, as the daylight began to fade into dusk, the Camerons and a few neighbours that they had called up set out to look for Marie. They whistled for her as they searched along the shore at Columba's Bay where she had often been seen writing while on the Island.

Darkness closed in, there were still no clues as to the whereabouts of Marie and the search had to be called off for the night. Search parties mustered with more islanders and the police from Mull (there were no police officers stationed on Iona) in the early hours of the following day and resumed when it got light on the cold and frosty morning of Tuesday, 19 November. Kitty Cameron made her way to the post office at Baile Mor and sent a telegram to Mrs Varney to inform her that Miss Fornario had gone out and had not returned. Kitty was probably hoping that Mrs Varney might have some clue as to where Marie might be, perhaps wondering if she had sent a telegram on Monday. Alas, Mrs Varney had last heard from her mistress in the letter that arrived a few days earlier in which Marie had said she might not hear from her for 'a long time' because she had 'a terrible healing case on'. Other than that, she was as much in the dark as the Camerons.

The search parties went over hill and ground to no avail through the morning.

Friends and fellow crofters Hector MacLean (65) of Sligneach and Hector MacNiven (43) of Maol Farm had been helping with the search parties but had to leave to attend to their livestock in the afternoon. At about 1.30 pm, the collie dog with them led the two Hectors over Staonaig, one of the rougher terrains of the island. There, on the lonely moor, they found Marie's naked dead body, lying cold and frozen in a hollow at the foot of Staonaig Hill.[13] A short distance away from her body lay a knife which had been used to cut out a large cross on the turf and the body rested on the sacred symbol. The only thing she was wearing was a silver cross on a chain. The crofters rushed to raise the alarm and police from the search parties were soon on the scene.

---

13. The location of body stated under 'When and Where Died' on Marie's Death Certificate.

Chapter 10

The Iona Mystery

Is this a dagger which I see before me …
William Shakespeare

Upon receiving the news of the discovery of the body, the policemen from Mull attended the scene and sent for a doctor. This was not a quick process on Iona in 1929 because no doctor was resident on the island, so he would have to travel over by boat or ferry from the Isle of Mull. The usual doctor who would attend sudden deaths, and indeed many other emergencies, was Dr Reginald Norman Macdonald (1877–1953) of Salen, a man remembered with great affection who would spend over 40 years on Mull.

In this instance, however, Dr Angus Matthew MacLeod, the locum at the surgery at Alva House, Bunessan, was sent to attend the scene. Dr MacLeod rapidly concluded the cause of death had been 'Exposure to the elements'.[1] In Scotland, there are no coroners. The Procurator Fiscal performs a similar role and it was a legal requirement that he be notified of any sudden deaths. Dr MacLeod would undoubtedly have informed Mr Donald Mackenzie MacKinnon, the long-standing Procurator-Fiscal for the County of Argyll in the Oban and Lorne Sheriff's Court district, accordingly.

The Glasgow-based *Daily Record* that proudly proclaimed itself 'Scotland's National Newspaper' was one of the first newspapers to report Marie's death on Wednesday, 20 November, the day after the discovery of her body. Published under the curious headline of 'Lost in Iona', there were a number of inaccuracies but the story was undoubtedly included in the paper in haste:

---

1. Extract of an entry from the *Register of Deaths in Scotland*: Death in the Parish of in the Parish of Kilfinichen and Kilvikeon in the County of Argyll, Norah Emily Edith Fornario, Registered 9 December 1929

Miss Farnario [*sic*], who had been staying at Traymore, Iona, for the winter, disappeared on Monday and search parties failed to find her. The police were summoned yesterday and discovered the body of the lady at Port Stonaig [sic]. Death was thought to be due to exposure.[2]

The *Glasgow Bulletin* would report a few days later:

The body was lying in a sleeping posture on the right side, the head resting on the right hand. Round the neck was a silver chain and cross. A few feet away a knife was found. Miss Farnario [sic] had left the Camerons' farmhouse (about a mile away) sometime during Sunday night. The island was bathed in moonlight and a very keen frost prevailed. The doctor who was called gave it as his opinion that death was due to exposure.

With the exception of a few scratches on the feet, caused by walking over the rough ground, there were no marks on the body.

The Oban Times, the newspaper local to Iona, was a weekly newspaper that went to press on Wednesdays ready for release on Saturdays. It first ran the story on 23 November:

Miss Farnario [sic], a visitor to Iona who had been staying at Traymore for the winter, disappeared on Monday and search parties failed to find her. The police were informed of the occurrence on Tuesday and during the afternoon the lady's body was discovered at Stonaig. Death was due to exposure.[3]

A number of British national newspapers, including *Reynolds's News*, *Daily Chronicle* and *Daily News*, picked up on the story, sent reporters to interview Mrs Varney and a number of Marie's neighbours and published features on their pages between 27 November and 1 December revealing more about her personal life as a faith healer, spiritualist and Theosophist, how she believed in fairies and 'dabbled in the occult'.[4] The story was

---

2. *Daily Record*, Wednesday 20 November 1929
3. *Oban Times and Argyllshire Advertiser*, 23 November 1929
4. *Daily Chronicle*, 27 November 1929

clearly capturing the public's interest and imagination and was soon appearing in various newspapers under the title of 'Iona Mystery'. On 28 November, a portrait photograph of Marie even made the front page of the *Daily Mirror*.

Unsurprisingly, the *Daily Record* and *The Scotsman* covered the story in some detail too. On 29 November, the *Daily Record* even published a recent photograph of Marie taken during her stay on Iona showing her in profile sat on a rocky bank, very much as locals would have often seen her when she was reading, writing and contemplating on the banks overlooking Columba's Bay. In the published photo, she appears to be taking a photograph with a Houghton-Butcher 'JB' Ensign or similar roll film box camera that were very popular at the time.

A number of provincial newspapers covered the story, including *The Herald*, a Richmond newspaper that was local to where Marie lived that ran the headline of 'Died on Lonely Island' on 30 November. The article described Marie as 'A Kew Woman Mystic' and published much the same content as the nationals, including the 'terrible healing case' letter and Mrs Varney's account of life with her mistress.

The Scotsman added some interesting details from Iona, where locals had talked to reporters and the police had begun enquiries and searched Marie's room:

Among weird stories now in circulation in island regarding Miss Fonario are mysterious remarks about blue lights having been seen near the body, and of a cloaked man. A number of letters, said to be of a strange character, have been taken possession of by the police, who, it is also stated, have passed them on to the Procurator-Fiscal for his consideration.[5]

The *Daily News* of 27 November claimed that the contents of these letters 'make remarkable assertions'.[6] The following day, the same newspaper included the detail that Mrs Varney had received a letter from Marie's 'landlady in Iona', presumably Kitty Cameron, saying 'the doctor there is of

---

5. *The Scotsman*, 27 November 1929
6. *Daily News*, 27 November 1929

the opinion that Miss Fornario died of heart failure'.[7] Had the newspaper made a mistake or was there really a conflict of medical opinion?

The Oban Times revisited the story on Saturday, 30 November but tucked away on page five, below articles on the condition of Scottish fisheries, the annual gathering of the Clan MacMillan Society, the Clan Cameron gathering in Glasgow and the detailed accounts of funerals, including a list of mourners for the late Mrs Thorpe of Ardbrecknish and a disputed rent action in Oban Sheriff's Court, was a two paragraph report under the heading of 'Fate of an Iona Visitor, London Woman Found Dead' that stated:

It now transpires that the woman who was found at Stonaig on Tuesday of last week, was Miss Nora Emily Fornario, Mortlake Road, Kew. The deceased who was a visitor to Iona and had been staying at Traymore for the winter, had disappeared on the previous Sunday. Her body, which was unclothed was discovered lying on a large cross which had been cut out of the turf, apparently with a knife which was lying by, and round her neck was a silver chain and cross. The remains were interred.[8]

The second paragraph mentions her being the daughter of an Italian doctor and 'was apparently a woman of extraordinary character'. Mentioning Mrs Varney, that article goes on to mention that Marie 'cured people by telepathy' and that she 'went into trances, and would remain in that condition for hours'.

Marie's funeral took place on Friday, 22 November and was well attended by the inhabitants of Iona. She was given the most honoured burial possible on the island in the Reilig Odhrán (St Oran's Chapel Cemetery), the sacred burial place of kings and highland chieftains. Her grave is marked by a small and simple but fitting stone carved in the form of a book, marked as she personalised her own books, with her initials M.E.F on the inside of the front cover:

7. *Daily News*, 28 November 1927
8. *Oban Times*, 30 November 1929

M.E.F.
                19th NOV. 1929
AGED 33

Her father did not make the journey to attend his only child's funeral, neither did her aunt and uncle, who had acted as her guardians and trustees as she grew up. In fairness to her father, the news of her death and hasty funeral may have arrived with him in Italy too late to make the journey. There is, however, no evidence to suggest he ever travelled to visit his daughter's grave. Everything was simply placed in the hands of a solicitor.

Armed with the letters found in her room and reports from the police and Dr MacLeod, Procurator Fiscal Donald MacKinnon made a special journey on 26 November to investigate the islanders' stories but Marie had already been buried before he had sight of her body. No file appertaining to her sudden death survives. The location of the letters passed to the Procurator Fiscal is unknown nor are any transcriptions or copies of them known to exist.

Molly Whittington-Egan, in her excellent account of the case in *Classic Scottish Murder Stories*, recounted:

I mentioned the case to our doctor friend, and, off the top of his head, he suggested poison, but, to my shame, I could not tell him if there had been a chemical analysis of the organs, and I was not even at all sure that there had been a post-mortem! He told me further, that a sound diagnosis of heart-failure cannot be based on external observation alone … the procurator fiscal for the district, if not satisfied with the findings of the doctor called to the scene, would have ordered a post-mortem.[9]

Molly and the Whittington-Egan's doctor friend were right. A subsequent check of records released to date in various Scottish archives, including the Lord Advocate's Department archives at the National Records of Scotland, during research for this book, has found no files referring to the death of Marie Fornario. There is no evidence to suggest Marie's body

---

9. Whittington-Egan, Molly, *Classic Scottish Murder Stories* (Wilson, 1999)

had been photographed by the police, no post-mortem appears to have been carried out save a visual examination by Dr MacLeod and there is no record of toxicology tests being conducted on her body.

A solicitor was despatched to deal with matters on behalf of Marie's family, so no family member formally identified the body as that of Marie. The delay of a few days does suggest some enquiries were carried out by Procurator Fiscal MacKinnon but, ultimately, if no locals or police raised sufficient concerns or suspicions, he would logically take Dr MacLeod's word for Marie's cause of death and he apparently dismissed the mysterious circumstances that surrounded it without having sight of the body himself.

Procurator Fiscal MacKinnon registered Marie's death with Mr Alexander M. MacGregor, the Assistant Registrar at Bunessan, Mull, on 9 December 1929. Recording her name as Norah Emily Edith Fornario (no mention of her first name of Marie), the cause of death was recorded as 'exposure to the elements' in accord with Dr MacLeod's opinion. Under when and where she died, he recorded it as 'Between 10 pm on 17 November and 1.30 pm on 19 November, body found on latter date on Staonaig Hill, Iona'. The entry was counter-signed as correct by the Registrar.[10]

On 5 December 1929, interest in the death of Marie Fornario was reignited by a strange tale first published in the *Daily News* under the headline of 'Death Message by Telepathy' and credited to Central News, Rome on 4 December, the article claims:

Professor Fornario, father of Miss Norah Emily Fornario of London, who died on Holy Island, off the West Coast of Scotland, on Nov. 19 states that he received a telepathic message of his daughter's death at the time of its occurrence.[11]

Knowing Marie's claimed abilities to be able to communicate telepathically, this story chimes well with the published narratives to date but a story published in the *Daily Express* on 5 December claiming to be from

---

10. Extract of an entry from the *Register of Deaths in Scotland*: Death in the Parish of in the Parish of Kilfinichen and Kilvikeon in the County of Argyll, Norah Emily Edith Fornario, Registered 9 December 1929

11. *Daily News*, 5 December 1929

one of their own correspondents ups the intrigue. Under the headline *Woman's Dread of a Statue: Death Follows Gift from Her Father*, a story dated 4 December, stated to have come from Marie's father, named in the paper as Dr Joseph Fornario from a correspondent in Rome, relates the tale of how:

A spiritual conflict had arisen between him and his daughter, principally on account of a statue of Osiris which he had given her when they were both in Egypt. Miss Fornario, who was interested in psychic phenomena, declared that the statue was evil, and would only bring misfortune. Her father, who is a noted scientist and a director of the Medical Institute at Milan, declined to admit this, and they argued heatedly on the matter.

Dr Fornario added that by some strange phenomena of telepathy he had the sensation that something terrible had happened to his daughter on the exact day which she died. He did not hear of her death until two days afterwards.[12]

Two days later, the story appears in the *Daily Mirror* attributed to John English, a regular reporter and feature writer for the *Mirror* in which he postulates:

Explorers and archaeologists are supposed to have been pursued by vindictive spirits. The record of ill-fortune attending members of the Tut-ankh Amen expeditions is enough to make one wonder whether the ancient Egyptian possessed powers that are unknown to us.

The account then ramps up the narrative, claiming the fatal effect of the statue to have taken place just weeks after it was given to Marie:

The latest extraordinary story regarding a statue of Osiris hails from Italy. A certain Dr Fornario presented his daughter with the relic. She is alleged to have had a presentiment that evil would result. Within a few weeks she was dead.[13]

---

12. *Daily Express*, 4 December 1929
13. *Daily Mirror*, 6 December 1929

The deadly Osiris statue story can, I think, be best described as 'creative journalism'. However, the notion of a curse, but not one from a statue or any elemental of ancient Egypt, attached to the death of Marie Fornario, may not entirely be misplaced. Mysterious blue lights, just the sort of lights long recorded in Iona and Hebridean folklore, were reportedly seen over where Marie's body was found and over her grave after her burial, adding to the mystery that surrounded her death. Historically, myths and faeries were also used to explain sudden deaths, possibly from heart attacks or witchcraft, to explain poisoning before science had advanced enough to test for poisons but what did those around in 1929 believe?

Those who may have failed Marie by not investigating her death as thoroughly as they possibly could certainly had untimely death and misfortune befall them. Procurator Fiscal MacKinnon had enjoyed an active life and good health but dropped down dead after a short illness, aged 59, less than two years later in July 1931.[14]

Dr Angus MacLeod resumed work back in Glasgow with his wife Margaret until 1933, when he was appointed the resident doctor for Dinnington Colliery, Northumberland. The position came with a house named 'Clairmont' and while they were there, they would be blessed with children Margaret and Donald. In the early hours of 26 October 1939, less than a month short of the tenth anniversary of Marie's death, a mysterious fire broke out in 'Clairmont' that could have wiped out Dr MacLeod and his family had it not been for the swift actions of their young servant, Miss Ella Grey (16). Ella slept in the same room as the two young children and she awoke to the smell and sound of the fire. She managed to get both children out and alerted Dr MacLeod. The doctor did awaken but he had been greatly affected by the smoke. He was able to get to the window and with the assistance of neighbours was able to reach safety.

Whether you consider there is something in the 'curse' on the Procurator Fiscal and the Doctor or not, many in the occult community, particularly those who knew Marie, were convinced that there had been something more to her sudden death. The following was published in the February 1930 edition of *The Occult Review*:

---

14. *Oban Times*, 1 August 1931

The mysterious death of a student of occultism, Miss N. Fornario, is receiving the attention of the authorities at the present time. Miss Fornario was found lying nude on the bleak hillside in the lonely island of Iona. Round her neck was a cross secured by a silver chain, and near at hand lay a large knife which had been used to cut a large cross in the turf. On this cross her body was found lying. A resident of London, Miss Fornario seems to have made her way to Iona for some purpose connected with occultism, one of the servants at her house in London stating that a letter had been received saying she had "a terrible healing case on." One newspaper report alludes to "mysterious stories on the island about blue lights having been seen in the vicinity of where her body was found, and there is also a story of a cloaked man." Occultists no less than the general public will await with interest any disclosures which may be forthcoming concerning the occurrence. The general impression is that Miss Fornario died from exposure. [15]

Violet Firth, writing as Dion Fortune in her book *Psychic Self-Defence: A Study in Occult Pathology and Criminality* (1930), added her perspective:

It is very necessary with so much occult knowledge about, that people should know an occult attack when they see it. These things are much more common than is generally realised. The recent tragedy in Iona gives point to this assertion. No occultist is under any illusion as to that death being from natural causes. In my own experience I have known of similar deaths …[16]

Firth concludes on the death of Marie:

She had evidently been on an astral expedition from which she never returned. She was not a good subject for such experiments, she suffered from some defect of the pituitary body. Whether she was the victim of a psychic attack, whether she merely stopped out on the astral too long and her body, of poor vitality in any case, became

---

15. *The Occult News*, Volume LI No. 2, February 1930
16. Fortune, Dion, *Psychic Self-Defence: A Study in Occult Pathology and Criminality* (Rider, 1930)

chilled lying thus exposed in mid-winter, or whether she slipped into one of the elemental kingdoms that she loved, even as Swinburne swam out to sea, who shall say. The information at our disposal is insufficient for an opinion to be formed. The facts, however, cannot be questioned, and remain to give sceptics food for thought.[17]

17. Fortune, Dion, *Psychic Self-Defence: A Study in Occult Pathology and Criminality* (Rider, 1930)

Chapter 11

The Beast 666

Let him who has understanding reckon the number of the beast, for it is a human number, its number is six hundred and sixty-six.

Revelation 13:18

Aleister Crowley was the most infamous occultist of the twentieth century. He was a man who styled himself as The Beast 666. He is best known for his prolific publishing on the occult and magickal rites. He always spelt magick with a 'k' to distinguish it from stage magic tricks. Crowley thrived on shock, awe and notoriety of the rumours and sensational revelations published in newspapers of his depraved rites and lifestyle. At the height of his infamy in the 1920s and early 1930s, Crowley was described in the press as 'The Wickedest Man in the World', *John Bull* newspaper even went so far as to declare him 'A Man We'd Like to Hang'. Death seemed to follow Crowley wherever he went. At times, he would claim it had been his spells and curses that had been responsible and he revelled in the aura and the power it gave him.

Unsurprisingly, Crowley has been mentioned in the lyrics of heavy metal bands and performers such as Iron Maiden and Ozzy Osbourne but Crowley was originally 'rediscovered' more subtlely in the 1960s and 70s as a rebel and counter-culture icon by the likes of Led Zeppelin's Jimmy Page, The Rolling Stones, The Doors and David Bowie. Crowley even appeared among the many notable and notorious faces on The Beatles' iconic *Sgt. Pepper's Lonely Hearts Club Band* album cover, created by artists Peter Blake and Michael Leeson. As a result, Crowley acquired a renewed cult status and in recent years his surname has been used for characters in modern TV series with occult themes and he has been the subject of revisionist histories that depict him as a much maligned and misunderstood genius.

Mystery always surrounded the death of Norah Fornario. There was mention of: 'mysterious stories on the island about blue lights having been seen in the vicinity of where her body was found' and 'a mysterious cloaked man' being spotted on the island at the time of her death. Not to mention the ritualistic elements of her being found dead naked lying on a cross cut in the ground with a knife.

The Occult Review report of her death stated: 'Occultists no less than the general public will await with interest any disclosures which may be forthcoming concerning the occurrence' and as we have seen Dion Fortune (Violet Firth) summed up the feeling among occult circles when she wrote in the preface for her book, *Psychic Self-Defence* (1930):

> The recent tragedy in Iona gives point to this assertion. No occultist is under any illusion as to that death being from natural causes. In my own experience I have known of similar deaths ...

In occult circles, there was no doubt the finger of suspicion was levelled at Aleister Crowley for involvement in the death of Norah Fornario. Many members of the public who had followed the stories of 'The Beast' in the press would draw similar conclusions from the moment the circumstances of how her body was found were reported and it was revealed she had been a student of the occult and a practicing member of secret magical societies in London.

At the time of Norah's death, Crowley had been a known figure on the occult scene for decades and I think it is worthwhile to tell some of the back story of this man, how he became so notorious and why he would have drawn such suspicion.

Aleister Crowley was born Edward Alexander Crowley to wealthy parents John and Emily Crowley at 30 Clarendon Square, Leamington Spa, Warwickshire, on 12 October 1876. His father was a trained engineer but his share in the family brewery, Crowley's Alton Ales, had enabled him to retire before Edward was born.

John and Emily were both members of the Christian fundamentalist Plymouth Brethren and brought up young Edward accordingly and sent him to The White Rock evangelical Christian 'boarding school for young gentlemen' on Pevensey Road, St Leonards on Sea, Hastings,

Sussex, run by H. T. Habershon, and then to Ebor preparatory school in Cambridge. Tragically, Crowley's father died from tongue cancer in 1887 when Edward was 11 years old and it had a profound effect on the boy and he began to rebel. The moralistic Christian teachers at his school became particular targets for young Crowley.

Education at that time was very much learn by rote but rather than putting up and shutting up as the lessons were drilled into him, Crowley dared to sceptically question inconsistencies in the Bible in the lessons where it was taught. Having been taught by rote themselves, his masters were often ill-prepared nor willing to discuss any challenge to what they were teaching and would rapidly resort to corporal punishments such as a strap or ruler whacked over the knuckles, or even a caning, to silence him and punish such insolence. Crowley soon formed the opinion from the punishments that he received from the Reverend Henry d'Arcy Champney, headmaster of Ebor School, that the man was a sadist.

As he matured, Crowley progressively transgressed the Christian morality drilled into him during his upbringing by flagrantly smoking and masturbating. He is known to have attended Malvern College and Eastbourne College and has the ignominious distinction of being expelled from Tonbridge after catching gonorrhoea from a prostitute. Crowley seldom stayed at any one school for long before he refused to return, his mother was asked to withdraw him or he was expelled.

The boy was clearly troubled, as well evinced by an incident he would recall in his writings when he heard that a cat was said to have nine lives. Crowley determined to see if the claim was true:

I caught a cat, and having administered a large dose of arsenic, 1 chloroformed it, hanged it above the gas jet, stabbed it, cut its throat, smashed its skull, and, when it had been pretty thoroughly burnt, drowned it and threw it out of the window that the fall might remove the ninth life. The operation was successful. I was genuinely sorry for the animal; I simply forced myself to carry out the experiment in the interests of pure science.

From the mid-1890s, Edward rebranded himself and began using the name Aleister instead of his birth name after forming the belief that a dactyl followed by a spondee in a first name conferred the greatest chance of becoming famous. One of the earliest appearances of him using the name appeared in a short-published correspondence in the sedate *Eastbourne Gazette* newspaper during August and September 1894. Crowley wrote in reply an article by 'Censor', the author of the *Musings by the Sea* column that nestled comfortably beside such columns as *Roundabout Notes* of 'local and county jottings' and *Police Intelligence*.

'Censor' had published an article expressing criticism and concern over the ever-increasing number of 'useless and needless climbs of Beachy Head' that 'Censor' argued were in danger of damaging the notable local promontory, not to mention the concern that with ever-growing numbers of those climbing the cliffs, the chances increased of a serious accident occurring that would have a detrimental effect on the holiday trade of the town as a whole.

At the time, Crowley was approaching his eighteenth birthday and was already an experienced and enthusiastic climber. His correspondence was measured but we can see something of 'The Beast' in his writing, as this excerpt demonstrates:

The climbing of chalk or anything else is utterly foolish where persons unaccustomed to, and ignorant of their task, undertake it. Criticism of such climbing by persons ignorant of the subject seems to be equally so. The photographs in Mr Gibb's window may appear to the uninitiated as representing perilous positions – to the mountaineer they are by no means such a character. Thousands of people consider cycling suicide and football felo de se, but even 'Censor's' eloquence would hardly convince the cyclist or the footballer.

The suggestion that the cliffs are marred by our 'pick-axes' as our weapons are quaintly mistermed, is surely rather grotesque, if not purile. Chatsworth is hardly defaced by the fall of one tree, nor is the midnight sky irretrievably ruined by the fall of one meteor. Besides, the weather. In a week, destroys more of the cliff than the united Alpine Club could possibly do in twenty years.

I must thank 'Censor' for terming me adventurous, even though in scorn. A study of history might reveal the fact that there was a time when a spice of British pluck was not held as either a vice or a folly. But I write, perhaps, of long past ages.

However, as 'Censor' truly says, there is a limit at which pluck becomes foolhardiness. It is the case when men without properly nailed boots, without ice-axes, without a rope and without any experience of rotten rock, attempt passages where there is the least danger to life and limb. But for those properly equipped I must maintain that climbing on Beachy Head is a most healthful exercise, and one beyond its physical effects – teaching pluck, nerve, coolness, steadiness, prudence and experience. It is the best possible training for the Alps etc since the chalk climber has to use such extreme care.

In conclusion, I regret that others should have been made so anxious – as I believe, unnecessarily – also that others should have been led to imitate my climbs without suitable precautions. Mountaineering taken lightly, and without a serious conception of the responsibility incurred, is alike insane and criminal ...[1]

The letter was signed 'E. Aleister Crowley', and if anyone had been in any doubt about his credentials as a climber, even after he had name-dropped The Alpine Club in his letter, he added the Hotel Sulden, Tyrol, Austria, as the return address.

The *Eastbourne Gazette* correspondence demonstrates something of the skilled manner in which Crowley framed his arguments and how, in this instance, he would attempt to stimulate the deep-seated aspirations that were to be admired in the British national psyche of the time, such as those of courage or 'pluck'. In doing this, he hoped to appeal to the readership and win support for his argument. It can also be seen how he acknowledges amateurs but warns that only those with the correct knowledge, equipment and experience should attempt such things, or they do so at their peril. Crowley would apply similar techniques to defend his actions and magickal practices over the years to come.

In 1895, Crowley was entered for the Moral Science Tripos at Trinity College, Cambridge. Safe in the knowledge that at the age of twenty-one he would inherit a large trust fund from his late father that would mean

---

1. *Eastbourne Gazette*, Wednesday 5 September 1894

he would never really need to work, Crowley spent the lion's share of his time indulging his pastimes instead of studies. Of his socially acceptable pursuits, Crowley excelled at chess, which he played to a masterful standard and would further his accomplishments as a mountaineer.

While at university, he also published his first poems but did so, having taken the precaution of publishing under a false name and abroad because they were so pornographic their publication would have been banned in Britain and he would have risked prosecution for obscenity. Indeed, the poems reveal some of Crowley's ever-growing and unhealthy obsession with sex, which he not only wrote about but indulged in on a regular basis with men and women, the latter mostly prostitutes from whom it was rumoured he contracted syphilis. This latter contention, undoubtedly based on his known sexual practices, has often been repeated but is yet to be confirmed from medical records.

While he was at Cambridge, Crowley became fascinated by the mysteries of the occult. He read widely and having learned of secret magical societies and the dark and forbidden rituals enacted by their members, he was desperate to obtain admission. In 1898, Crowley was particularly delighted to obtain Arthur Edward Waite's privately printed *The Book of Black Magic and of Pacts* which proudly announced by way of subtitle that it included the *Rites and Mysteries of Goetic Theurgy, Sorcery, and Infernal Necromancy.*

Crowley made sure he made the right contacts and within a few months of leaving university, he was initiated into the Outer Order of The Hermetic Order of the Golden Dawn by the group's leader, Samuel Liddell MacGregor Mathers, at the Isis-Urania Temple meeting held at Mark Masons Hall on St James's Street, London on 18 November 1898. Crowley chose the name Perdurabo (which means 'I will endure until the end') by which he would be known in the Order.

At the time Crowley was admitted to the Isis-Urania Temple, its members included professionals in law, medicine and the arts. Among them were the author Arthur Machen, Arthur Edward Waite (Sacramentum Regis), the author of *The Book of Black Magic* that had so intrigued Crowley and the artist Pamela 'Pixie' Colman Smith (Quod Tibi Id Allis) who, with Waite, were two of the three creators of the Rider-Waite-Smith Tarot deck. There was Florence Farr (Sapientia Sapienti Dono Data), actress and author of the books *Egyptian Magic* and *The Dancing Faun*; the actress and suffragette Maude Gonne (Per Ignem Ad Lucem), and the poet W B Yeats (Demon Est Deus Inversus) who described the Golden Dawn both as 'his church and his university'.

The entree to this elite, deeply cultured and talented group of aesthetes should have been more than enough for anyone, but not Crowley, who rapidly came to the conclusion his fellow members of the Temple did not immerse themselves in learning the rituals as he did, nowhere near.

Crowley constructed a private temple in his flat in Chancery Lane. He would describe it as 'a hall of mirrors, the function of which was to concentrate the invoked forces. It contained an altar of acacia topped with gold and certain secret symbols and regalia of the Orde..'

Crowley would write evocatively of just how powerful the magick in the temple he created could be:

One night, after a ceremony in which a well-known analytical chemist was my leader, I locked the door and went out with him to a meal. When we returned the door was wide open, though the lock had not been forced, and the whole contents of the temple had been thrown about and lay in the wildest confusion. Then the fun began. We saw – and my teacher was able to identify hundreds of shapes, weird "half-formed faces" which were thronging the room, marching in fantastic dance about its confines. These were definitely malicious forces, demons, which one had to study and conquer.

Later, when I was transferring my apparatus to my house in Scotland. I employed two workmen to remove the mirrors. As they were working they were suddenly overcome, knocked-out by unseen assailants. It took several hours to revive them. People passing the doorway suddenly fell down in fits. That flat remained without a tenant for years after I had left it. All this was because I had not enough experience to control the forces.[2]

Golden Dawn leader MacGregor Mathers was translating an ancient text for a magical system said to have been taught by an Egyptian mage named

---

2. *Weekly Dispatch*, 25 June 1933

Abraham, or Abramelin to Abraham of Worms who, in turn, passed it on his son in the fifteenth century. In this magical system was a certain rite described in the translation as an 'Operation', which if completed properly and successfully, would reward the magician by enabling him to achieve communion with his Holy Guardian Angel. Having reached the Guardian Angel over the next three days, the successful performer of the rite would be required to summon and bind the twelve Kings and Dukes of Hell: Satan, Lucifer, Leviathan, Belial, Oriens, Amaymon, Paimon, Ariton, Asmodee, Belzebub, Magot, and Astaroth. These demons and their subservient spirits could bestow an amazing array of hidden knowledge and powers from shape-shifting, walking on water, healing the sick and even destroying enemies.

Unsurprisingly, the preparations for the person attempting the rite and the chance to obtain the fabulous powers it offered were no mean feat. It would entail the conversion of rooms in a house specifically for the purpose of performing the rite and a period of personal preparation involving purification, celibacy, and abstinence from alcohol for a period of six months, culminating in an arduous seven-day long ritual.

Mathers' translation was published as *The Sacred Magic of Abramelin the Mage* by the London esoteric book dealer and publisher John M. Watkins of 26 Charing Cross Road in 1898. Late in 1899, Crowley bought Boleskine House on the bucolic banks of Loch Ness, in Foyers, Aberdeenshire, Scotland.

Crowley had no Scottish ancestry of his own but soon immersed himself deeply in the land and its traditions wearing highland dress as his day-to-day garb complete with kilt, plaid and glengarry even when he was in London. He adopted the name Aleister Crowley MacGregor, possibly in a nod to MacGregor Mathers, not to mention it is a good Scottish name that would enhance Crowley's new Scottish identity, but he did not stop there.

In accordance with the old Scottish practice of calling a landowner a laird, Crowley was soon styling himself 'Laird of Boleskine'. A term Crowley chose to interpret more as a lord of nobility rather than landlord and accordingly had a coronet embossed on his notepaper, with a gilt B (for Boleskine) underneath and even a coat of arms, with an aphorism in Sanskrit thrown in for good measure on his letterhead.

Above all, Crowley had acquired Boleskeine because he considered it a uniquely suitable property and location to work the Abramelin Operation and paid £2000 for the house, twice its market value at the time, to own it. In *The Great Beast*, Crowley's literary executor, John Symonds, explained:

If you wish to perform the operation of conjuring up your Holy Guardian Angel, says the magician Abra-Melin, you must first of all construct an oratory in a secluded spot. This oratory, or temple, should have a door opening northwards onto a terrace covered with fine river sand. At the end of the terrace there should be a lodge where the evil spirits (who can be approached safely only after the Holy Guardian Angel has been invoked) may congregate. For they are prohibited in the oratory. And this lodge should have windows on all sides so that the demons therein may be seen more easily.

Crowley would claim in his own account of his life published in the *Weekly Dispatch* in 1933:

It was at the direction of the head of the Order [MacGregor Mathers] that I then went to Scotland to my manor house of Boleskine … My subsidiary object – the principal aim is too sacred to discuss – put into simple language, was to gain control over the 'four great princes' of the evil of the world.

But of course, Crowley did not explain what he intended to do if he did successfully gain control of these demons. It is hard to believe Crowley would have waited for the command of Mathers to undertake the Abramelin operation. Once he heard of it, he would have wanted to be the first to achieve it. Crowley went on to explain:

According to the rules of magic, I built a terrace with a northern aspect and carted river-sand to it. I worked in the breakfast-room at making the talismans which were necessary to my purpose. The sun was streaming into the room, but in vain; there was a darkness which could be felt. The demons, evil forces, had congregated round me so thickly that they were shutting off the light. It was a comforting situation. There could be no more doubt of the efficiency of the operation.

But I went on with my work, even though I had to light a lamp – with the sun shining brightly outside. The demons collected, also, in the lodge which I had built on the terrace. They were still vague shapes, half-seen faces. I got used to them.

They had curious effects on the neighbourhood. Part of the main road from Inverness to Fort Augustus ran through my estate. Soon superstitions about the road made the natives avoid it. People refused to use it after nightfall. Even the tough, hard-drinking workmen from Glasgow who were employed at Foyers would go a long way round to avoid that uncanny road.

The forces had other and worse effects. An employee (who had not touched alcohol for 20 years) suddenly got drunk and tried to murder his wife and children. This was one of many similar cases. One summer more than half my pack of bloodhounds died. My servants were always getting ill. One of the men I employed to lay down putting-greens went insane and tried to murder my wife. I had realised, by time, that my path to power was to be immensely difficult and fraught with danger. But I did not look back.[3]

Symonds published further revelations in *The Great Beast*:

Crowley successfully raised them [the demons] 'the lodge and the terrace,' he wrote, 'soon became peopled with shadowy shapes,' – but he was unable to control them. Oriens, Paimon, Ariton, Amaimon, and their hundred and eleven servitors escaped from the lodge, entered the house and wrought havoc: his coachman, hitherto a teetotaller, fell into delirium tremens; a clairvoyante whom he had brought from London returned there and became a prostitute; his housekeeper, 'unable to bear the eeriness of the place', vanished; a madness settled upon one of the workmen employed on the estate and he tried to kill the Laird of Boleskine.

---

3. *Weekly Dispatch,* Sunday 25 June 1933

Even the butcher down in the village was affected through Crowley's casually jotting down on one of his bills the names of two demons, viz. Elerion and Mabakiel, which mean respectively 'laughter' and 'lamentation'. Conjointly these two words signify 'unlooked-for sorrow suddenly descending upon happiness'. Alas, only too true, for while cutting up a joint for a customer, the butcher accidentally severed his femoral artery and promptly died.

Back in the Isis-Urania Temple in London, Crowley had made himself deeply unpopular among the members because of his overbearing and sneering attitude towards any member he did not consider was taking the rituals as seriously as he did. There also appears to have been a police investigation of some homosexual conduct at Cambridge involving Crowley (homosexual acts between men were a criminal offence in Britain until 1967).

Nothing appears to have come of the matter but any whiff of scandal, in addition to his pornographic publications and his lewd conversation experienced by members of the Temple, were reasons enough for them to distance themselves from Crowley and he was refused initiation into the Second Order. Crowley would claim in *Confessions*, that fellow Temple member Isabel Simpson (the mother of Elaine Simpson, also a member of the Temple whom Crowley would describe as his 'Mistress') had told him the members of the Second Order had voted to refuse to initiate him after he had been suspected of using the sex act to gain magical power.

Undoubtedly feeling more than a sense of entitlement to progress in the Golden Dawn, Crowley approached MacGregor Mathers directly and despite having spent months in preparation for the Abramelin process, he dropped it and travelled to Paris where Mathers personally admitted Crowley into the Adeptus Minor Grade. Mathers' autocratic decisions and leadership had become increasingly unpopular over time and had already caused rifts in the Golden Dawn. The admission of Crowley to the Adeptus proved to be the last straw, especially when, by return, Mathers dispatched the newly elevated Crowley to London as his envoy with a statement that he expected all adepts of the Isis-Urania Temple to sign pledging allegiance to Mathers.

In collusion with fellow member Elaine Simpson, Crowley and Simpson blagged their way in past the landlord, Mr Wilkinson, forced the door of the Temple on the first floor of 36 Blythe Road, West Kensington and changed the locks in an attempt to prevent other members entering. Attempting to hide his identity by conducting all correspondence under the guise of 'Envoy', Crowley summoned the Adepts of the Second Order to their Temple for individual interviews to establish their loyalty to Mathers and to sign the pledge document accordingly on 19 April 1900.

A printed statement of the subsequent events that occurred on 19 April was sent out to all Second Order Adepts of Isis Urania that recorded:

He [Crowley] arrived in Highland dress, a black mask over his face, a plaid thrown over his head and shoulders, an enormous gold or gilt cross on his breast, and a dagger at this side. All of this melodramatic nonsense was of course designed in the hope that it would cause members to sign a pledge … [Crowley] being unable to interview the members, who declined to be frightened by his mask and the rest of his childish make-up, caused a circular to be printed. Still not disclosing his identity with 'Envoy' and containing the following statement:- 'It should be mentioned that the story of the masked man is altogether untrue'.

Some of those present would tell, and legend would magnify the tale of how Yeats and Crowley embarked on a magical dual casting spells upon each other to yield while Yeats biographer Richard Ellman claims as Crowley continued to ascend to the first floor, '… *When Crowley came within range the forces of good [Edmund Hunter and Yeats] struck out with their feet and kicked him downstairs*'.

Crowley was then intercepted by the landlord and compelled to leave with the assistance of a police officer who had been summoned to the incident. Ultimately, Crowley was on a fool's errand in attempting to seize the Isis-Urania Temple because his name was not on the lease.

Crowley was expelled from the Golden Dawn, so he embarked upon his own odyessy in pursuit of enlightenment of the occult. He travelled and on arriving in Paris in 1902, he caught up with Gerald Kelly (Grandson of Frederic Festus Kelly, the founder of Kelly's Directories) who had known

Crowley during his first term at Cambridge. Through Kelly, Crowley had his entree to the artistic scene of the city. Crowley was introduced to Kelly's sister, the actress Rose Edith Kelly and swept her off her feet, the pair eloped and they married on 12 August 1903 to allegedly save her from an arranged marriage.

At least, that is one of the stories. Somerset Maugham met Crowley in Paris and has left an insight into the impression he made upon him:

I took an immediate dislike to him, but he interested and amused me. He was a great talker and he talked uncommonly well. In early youth, I was told, he was extremely handsome, but when I knew him he had put on weight, and his hair was thinning. He had fine eyes and a way, whether natural or acquired I do not know, of so focusing them that, when he looked at you, he seemed to look behind you … He was a liar and unbecomingly boastful, but the odd thing was that he had actually done some of the things he boasted of.

Maugham's most telling observation is the same one that many of those who met Crowley would make: 'He was a fake, but not entirely a fake'. Maugham would endow the character Oliver Haddo with most of the physical attributes and both the odious and magnetic character traits of Crowley in his novel *The Magician* (1908). A tale where a young couple were destined to be until Haddo came into their lives.

Edith joined Crowley in his travels and his occult pursuits and bore him two daughters. Firstborn was the charmingly named Nuit Ma Ahathoor Hecate Sappho Jezebel Lilith in 1904 (one does wonder how much say her mother had in naming her daughter). Tragically, Lilith died of typhoid while travelling with her family in Rangoon, India, in 1906. When the couple were in Hong Kong, Crowley abandoned Edith and instructed her to return directly to England while he planned to return via America. They were blessed with another daughter, Lola Zaza, in 1907 but Crowley met the poet Victor Neuburg. The pair began an affair in 1908 and Alaistair and Edith divorced in 1909. Crowley had Edith committed to Colney Hatch in 1911 on grounds of her 'alcohol dementia' and Lola ended up living with Edith's brother, Gerald.

In 1910, Crowley had established himself back in London and had taken a studio flat at 124 Victoria Street. A feature in *John Bull* sums Crowley up well:

A "new religion" is usually viewed with suspicion in this country, but Mr. Crowley is just the person for such an enterprise. He is a man of good birth and education, with distinguished, almost pontifical, manners. He has travelled over all the unusual parts of the world and investigated fantastic things with zeal, if not with discretion. He has probed the secret recesses of most Oriental religions and has made a special study of all the endless literature of magic and mysticism.

Though he has never yet succeeded in catching the long ear of the public, he has been a voluminous writer, and has published works which fill many shelves. "Konx Om Pax" and " 777" have already been noticed in this journal. To the uninitiated, they appear like the outpourings of an extremely clever lunatic, now solemnly revealing the secrets of the ancients, now running off into the most delightful nonsense, now assuming the role of the preacher, now frankly pulling legs. His chief efforts have been concentrated upon the composition of really remarkable poetry. His rhythm and metre and melody are often quite perfect, and as a lord of language he runs Swinburne very close. Often he goes very near to the borderland of insanity. His work, however, is spoiled by the intrusion of wild, erotic, and disgusting images and startling blasphemies, which restrict his writing to private circulation, though it possesses an artistic enchantment quite apart from its appeal to pruriency and debauchery.

His present 'mission' was heralded in March of last year by a portly publication called 'The Equinox'. The idea, evidently, is to attract the public to the teachings of medieval alchemists or magicians. The propaganda consists in assembling a number of ladies and gentlemen in a dark room, where poems are recited in sonorous tones and a violin is played with considerable expression, amid choking clouds of incense, varied by barbaric dances, sensational interludes of melodrama, blasphemy and erotic suggestion. [4]

---

4. *John Bull*, Saturday 05 November 1910

By this time, Crowley had taken a talented young violinist Leila Waddell as his mistress and developed a ritual around her playing. 'Vicky' Neuburg would dance and spin 'like a Devish' as Crowley provided the narration. These three were joined by theatrically minded accomplices for performances and intrigued guests could attend at the flat for the grand sum of £5 (about £500 in today's money). An investigative reporter recorded his experiences at one of the rituals held at the Victoria Street flat in 1910. Let's join him:

By special favour, or good fortune, or both, I was able to get free admission into the chamber of mysteries, which others less fortunate than I could not enter without paying in- advance a fee of £5. In the corridor there stood none other than Aleister Crowley himself – a man of fine physique and with all the appearance of an actor – in a long white garment, which reminded one of a cassock one moment and a Roman tunic the next, although undoubtedly it was neither the one nor the other. He vanished as mysteriously as he had appeared: Then there came among us, for a few, brief seconds, a woman, young, with strong features set in a deathly pale face. Someone said, "That is Lelia Waddell. She plays the violin and takes the chief part in the mystic seance."

A few of my own sex, in evening frocks, some looking as though they were strangers in the place, were enquiring for the dressing-room, and were informed there was only one such room, used by both sexes. A figure in a brown, monk-like frock, with face completely hidden by a cowl, passed among us, handing around type-written sheets explanatory of the performance, and then it was time to visit the mystic chamber.

The room was in semi-darkness, a bluish light hanging from the ceiling at the far end, a heavy smell of incense pervading the air, while the solemn stillness and hushed voices helped to enhance the weirdness of the place. I was taken to the front row, and a large cushion was given me to sit on. There were evidently no rules as to the pose one should adopt, for during the evening I saw some very Bohemian attitudes. To say the least, the cushions were not conducive to comfort, but those people behind me fared worse still. They sat on low wicker and bamboo footstools; several of these gave way during the performance, letting the unsuspecting occupants down, and not too gently!

Presently the door was closed and locked, the low blue light fell pale and mystical upon a male figure sitting behind a cauldron, with a drum between his knees; he beat the drum with his hands, paused, and then resumed the beating, and from a small door behind him entered a number of male and female figures, ten or twelve, clothed some in white, some in brown. He ceased to beat the drum, and one of the male figures then performed the vanishing ritual of the Pentagram, which is designed to keep away evil influences. He then lighted a fire in the cauldron, and, crouching behind, recited.

Next, he joined with the brethren in an endeavour to rouse someone whom they called the "Master of the Temple. I could not refrain from a feeling of envy at his ability to slumber through such a din! They failed to wake him, and the same brother appealed to the "Mother of Heaven." She appeared in the person of Lelia Waddell, played an invocation, and the "Master of the Temple" was at last aroused. I was not surprised!

He came forward, crouched behind the cauldron, and recited a most blood-curdling composition, filled with horrible allusions to "the stony stare of dead men's eyes," &c., &c. After all, one couldn't blame him for getting angry at being disturbed, I suppose. However, suddenly he lifted what looked like a tin of Nestle's milk, and pouring the contents on the flame, extinguished the fire, declared that "there is no God," that everybody was free to do just as he or she liked, and left the audience in utter darkness! Not the slightest ray of light entered the room, and the atmosphere seemed heavier and more oppressive than ever. There was a sound as of people moving quietly about, which added to the uncanniness. How long this lasted I do not know, but all of a sudden an arm was placed round my neck, and a moustache pressed to my cheek – . someone had kissed me!

The next moment the blue light appeared. The mystical figures were moving before me, and I watched, fascinated. The presence of a traitor among them was suspected, and a man clad in white, sword in hand, sought this traitor among the crouching figures. What a weird picture it was! With an unearthly scream he sprang upon one of the male figures, and, dragging him forth, "slew" him before our eyes. After this there was more violin music, and a wild barbaric dance in the misty, smoky blue light. One little scene that chilled my blood when the lights were extinguished. In the utter darkness, and after a long pause, in which one could hear one's own heart beat, a male voice, a terrible voice, called out: "My brethren, are the dead men fed?" "Yea, verily, the dead men are fed," came the reply. "My brethren, upon what have the dead men fed?" "Upon the corpses of their children" was the horrible answer. I had had enough, and was heartily glad when it was all over.

The ritual became so popular Crowley scripted and staged seven performances of *The Rites of Eleusis* at Caxton Hall. It certainly drew in the curious crowds but was condemned in some reviews as blasphemous and the *Looking Glass* went as far as to suggest that 'sexual irregularities' had occurred in the semi-darkness. One of the dancers hired for the performances was Ione de Forest (21), (real Mrs Jeanne Eugenie Merton née Heyse), described by Neuburg's biographer and friend Jean Overton-Fuller as 'a young girl of unearthly pallor; a fillet of silver leaves crowned her dark hair which fell loose about her form, robed in shining white. She was the moon'. Dame Rebecca West remembered her well as a fellow student at the Royal Academy of Dramatic Art in 1910:

She had a beautiful face of the Russian ballet type, oval with beautifully defined eyebrows; her hair was very black and her skin white. Most girls at that time did not use powder but a curious thing called papier poudre, and we thought it rather dashing of her to use powder – and terribly dashing when she took to using a pale blue or pale green powder to intensify the whiteness of her skin. This she had been taught to do by a famous beauty of the time … a poor girl who was just too marvellous to look upon … Her delivery was wooden and her movement stiff. She was also quite stupid on general matters. But her beauty was extraordinary, and she was sweet natured … She was not in the least what one would have expected from the daughter of a man who kept a lodging house in the Brixton Road …[5]

5. Fuller, Jean Overton, *The Magical Dilemma of Victor Neuburg* (Revised Edition), (Mandrake, 1990)

Ione and Neuburg became close but she married wealthy young engraver Gerald Merton in December 1911. Far from being a newcomer to the circle, Merton had known Neuburg when they were at Cambridge and had helped to finance the publication of Neuburg's first book, *The Green Garland* (1908). Merton's parents were Theosophists and were acquainted with the Russian-born mystic Helena Blavatsky, who was one of the co-founders of the Theosophical Society in 1875.

After just six months of marriage, Iona left the marital home at Cardinal Mansions, Chelsea, moved in to the Rossetti Studio on Flood-street, still in Chelsea, and took up with Neuburg. For his part, Neuburg hired a cottage in Essex where they could spend weekends together. Gerald Merton instituted divorce proceedings soon afterwards.

During the time Ione and Neuburg were a couple, they became friendly with a young artist named Nina Hamnett (22). Nina was a true bohemian and moved among the heart of the artist community of London at the time. She would recall Neuburg and Ione with affection but, curiously, she did not name them in her memoirs:

I was introduced one day to a poet. He had long hair. He lived with an extremely beautiful girl who was an actress. She had golden eyes and the most perfect eyebrows; she had long black hair down to her waist. He wrote hundreds and hundreds of poems to her. She had plenty of money always ...[6]

In turn, Neuburg would introduce Nina to Crowley at his studio. Crowley asked her to paint four panels with signs representing the elements for him at his flat which she did but, in doing so, she was aware of his reputation that he was 'so wicked that no young thing could remain alone in the same room with him in safety'. Nina did find herself alone with Crowley when his secretary popped out and according to her memoirs he simply laid on his hearth rug asleep, woke once, stared at her, asked, 'Are you alone?' and went back to sleep again.[7]

Curiously, Ethel Archer would describe to Jean Overton-Fuller how she had seen Ione standing behind Crowley's chair as he sat at a table, running

6. Hamnett, Nina *The Laughing Torso* (Constable, 1932)
7. Hamnett, Nina *The Laughing Torso* (Constable, 1932)

her hands through his hair and calling him 'Aleister'. Very few called him 'Aleister!' she proclaimed to emphasise 'the enormity of the familiarity' that was so striking to her. Hayter Preston, another of Neuburg's friends, was even of the opinion that Crowley had been intimate with Ione before Neuberg! He had met Crowley through Neuburg and could not reconcile Victor's association 'with a man whose sense of humour was so puerile'. Preston did not hide his contempt for Crowley, who he found 'vulgar, course, overwhelmingly conceited and fake'.[8]

Nina Hamnett recalled visiting Iona and Neuburg at the Rossetti Studio regularly, but all did not end well:

> I visited the poet and the beautiful girl quite often. She had a big studio in Chelsea. She seemed often depressed and one day said to me, I am going
>
> away to-morrow for a long time, perhaps for ever, come in the morning and I will give you some clothes. I was delighted as I had very few clothes.
>
> I felt rather worried about her but did not know what I could do. The next day I went to the studio. Outside pinned on the door was an envelope and inside was the key. I was rather frightened. I opened the door and inside was a large red curtain. I hesitated for a moment, terrified; I pulled it aside and on the sofa she lay dead, with a mother-o'-pearl revolver and her slippers beside her on the floor.[9]

The circumstances of Ione's suicide were utterly tragic. Nina would be called to give evidence at the inquest of the Coroner's Court for what was dubbed in the press as 'The Chelsea Studio Tragedy'. Stating she had known Iona for about six months, newspapers accounts of Nina's testimony related:

> It was only two months ago she learned she [Ione] was married. The witness added that Mrs Merton who was often melancholy, was studying painting. On Thursday the witness received a wire from her, and in response she went to Rossetti Studio. Mrs Merton was

---

8. Fuller, Jean Overton, *The Magical Dilemma of Victor Neuburg* (Revised Edition), (Mandrake, 1990)
9. Hamnett, Nina, *The Laughing Torso* (Constable, 1932)

particularly cheerful, said she was going away and gave the witness a letter to be opened at eleven o'clock next day. When the witness called on Friday at about eleven o'clock in the morning she found an envelope containing the key pinned to the door. Mrs Merton was lying on the divan, and she ran out and informed the caretaker.[10]

The evidence presented at the inquest also revealed Ione had written a final note to her estranged husband, which she posted to him. It simply stated: 'You have killed me. Jeanne'. Her husband, Wilfred Merton, an engraver, spoke of how Ione's health had been 'erratic' and how she 'was nervous and highly strung and subject to fits of hysteria' adding 'She had suggested suicide, but that was not taken seriously. She was not quite normal, and had threatened to take chloroform'.[11]

When she arrived on Friday at 11, Nina had found another envelope addressed to herself pinned to the outside of the door of the studio containing the key. The envelope given to Nina by Ione had been in a sealed envelope marked 'To be opened if I cannot see you at 11 o'clock on Friday mornin..' She left it to the Coroner to open it. Inside were two items: the certificate of marriage between Joan and Wilfred Merton and a gun licence issued to Joan, in the name of de Forest, on July 18, at Sloane Square. There was also a letter addressed to the coroner and it was read out in the court:

No. 5, Cardinal Mansions, August 1st
Last statement of Jeanne Merton wife of Wilfred Merton, of above address, written at her present residence, Rossetti Studio, where she has been living under her professional name of Ione de Forest, I hereby state that, although of sound mind, I intend committing suicide to-night because of the unbearable position which my extremely rash and unfortunate marriage has placed me in. It is my wish that my body be cremated.

Dr W E Robinson, of King's Road, Chelsea, stated the cause of death had been from syncope through a bullet wound in the heart. He also stated that he was 'satisfied the wound was self-inflicted, and that the

---

10. *Leeds Mercury*, 5 August 1912
11. *Leeds Mercury*, 5 August 1912

revolver was fired by a person who knew exactly where to shoot.' The jury returned a verdict of 'Suicide during temporary insanity'.[12]

Curiously, all the newspaper reports recorded Nina's name as Lena Hamnet, curiouser still Crowley, who had remained a friend of Hamnett for years afterwards, would make an extremely dark claim about the cause of Ione's death in his book *Magick in Theory and Practice* (1929):

> One may fascinate and bend to one's will a person who has of his own right the power to destroy. One may employ spirits or talismans. The more powerful magicians of the last few centuries have employed books.
>
> In private matters these Works are very easy, if they be necessary. An adept known to The Master Therion once found it necessary to slay a Circe who was bewitching brethren. He merely walked to the door of her room, and drew an Astral T ('traditore' and the symbol of Saturn) with an astral dagger. Within 48 hours she shot herself.

Neuburg had not been present at the inquest. He had been at their Essex cottage and would only discover what had happened after she didn't turn up. He was heartbroken by the suicide of Iona but he and Crowley carried on their relationship and the pair went to Paris in 1914, where they indulged themselves in extended drug-fuelled rituals. What exactly took place or had been said between the pair is unclear but the relationship ended soon afterwards.

Perhaps Crowley had made the claim, probably with some self-satisfaction, that it was his magick that had killed Ione and accused Neuburg of being the one who had cursed her to her doom. A nasty 'friend of a friend' rumour went around that Ione had killed herself after Neuburg 'had been cruel to her under the influence of the god Mars'. Or perhaps Crowley spitefully claimed he had primed Gerald Merton, the wrong husband, with the necessary curse to kill Ione. Either way when the story appeared in Crowley's *Magick in Theory and Practice* (1929), it was not Crowley but 'an Adept' known to him who 'slayed' her. It was an incredibly vitriolic thing to write and very typical of Crowley.

If Ione's suicide had been influenced by Crowley, or his magick, she was probably not the first nor would she be the last to suffer.

---

12. *Leeds Mercury*, 5 August 1912

Chapter 12

Wicked Recklessness

One may smile, and smile, and be a villain.
William Shakespeare

Crowley spent the First World War in the comparative safety of America, where he claimed Irish ancestry, publicly proclaimed himself a supporter of Irish independence, became involved in the pro-German movement in New York and indulged in anti-British propaganda as a writer for *The Fatherland* newspaper.

The *Sunday Express* regaled British audiences with an overview of Crowley's machinations while in the United States:

In November 1914 Crowley went to the United States, where he entered into close relations with the pro-German propagandists. He edited the New York "International," a German propagandist paper run by the notorious George Silvester Viereck, and published, among other things, an obscene attack on the King and a glorification of the Kaiser. Crowley ran occultism as a side line, and seems to have been known as the 'Purple Priest.' Later on he publicly destroyed his British passport before the Statue of Liberty, declared in favour of the Irish Republican cause, and made a theatrical declaration of 'war' on England. According to another version of this story he proclaimed himself at the same time 'King of Ireland.'

Revisionist historians have published tales of Crowley actually being a spy for British intelligence at the time, engaged in the penetration of anti-Britain factions in the United States. Intelligence services and Special Branch would undoubtedly have had files on Crowley and his activities. These files may or may not have been destroyed but the absence of solid evidence confirming Crowley acted as a spy for the British, emerging from any of the British intelligence services files released to the National Archives to date, provides no evidence to mitigate Crowley's actions.

Crowley never hid his disdain for the remaining members of the Golden Dawn and even began to mistrust Mathers, who he suspected was using magic against him and their friendship dissolved. When writing *The Confessions of Aleister Crowley: An Autohagiography* in the 1920s, he reflected on the aftermath of his dismissal from the Golden Dawn and the years afterwards and vented:

> They [the remaining members of the Golden Dawn] went on squabbling amongst themselves for a few months and then had the sense to give up playing at Magick. Their only survivor is Arthur Edward Waite, who still pretends to carry on the business, though he has substituted a pompous, turgid rigmarole of bombastic platitudes for the neophyte ritual, so that the last spark of interest is extinct for ever. Mathers, of course, carried on; but he had fallen. The Secret Chiefs cast him off; he fell into deplorable abjection; even his scholarship deserted him. He published nothing new and lived in sodden intoxication till death put an end to his long misery.

Mathers had also been expelled from the Golden Dawn in April 1900 but would form a new group in Paris in 1903 called Alpha et Omega that adopted the ritual magic and ceremonies of the Golden Dawn in all but name. MacGregor Mathers died in November 1918. He is believed to have been one of the millions of victims of the Spanish flu epidemic that swept across Europe at the end of the war. Even though Crowley was in America at the time, his literary executor and biographer John Symonds would record 'it was said that Crowley killed him'.[1] Nobody was saying Crowley had physically carried out the murder but there was a lot of talk at that time and throughout the 1920s of astral travel and Crowley would claim on numerous occasions that he could summon inviable assailants and even make himself invisible.[2]

Alpha et Omega would be carried on in Britain by his wife Moina Mathers and it would be this group that Theodore Moriarty, Violet

---

1. Symonds, John, *The Great Beast* (Rider, 1951)
2. *Weekly Dispatch,* Sunday 25 June 1933

Firth (Dion Fortune) and Norah Fornario, who adopted the name of Mac Tyler, would all be initiated and become active members. Crowley damned them all as only 'playing' at the rituals and embarked upon his own odyssey of personal enlightenment, creating his own groups on his own terms.

Crowley returned to London in late 1919 but soon baled over to France and rented a house at 11-bis rue de Neuville, Fontainebleau, with his new mistress Leah Hirsig, who soon fell pregnant. Crowley and Hirsig met young widow Ninette Shumway (born Augustine Louise Helene Fraux) on a ship during one of their trips to England and she joined them as a housekeeper to assist with things when the baby was born. Leah gave birth to Anne 'Poupée' Leah Crowley on 26 January 1920. Around this time, Crowley and Ninette became lovers.

Crowley wanted to form his own community of Thelemites and before 1920 was over, with mystical guidance, he decided to create his Abbey of Thelema at the old Villa Santa Barbara at Cefalù in Sicily. Sounds grand but it was single storey, rustic (and not in a charming way) and unsanitary to say the least. Separated from the town, it was a place where the distant bark of dogs was often to be heard but no one would hear you scream. Nonetheless, others would soon join them, including the American silent film actress, Jane Wolfe.

Everyone fell ill at the 'Abbey' at one time or another. Baby Poupée had not fared well at all and had been very ill. Sadly, she died on 14 October 1920. At the time, Leah was already a few months pregnant again but would suffer a miscarriage less than a week later. In November, Ninette was around eight months pregnant with Crowley's baby when Leah and Crowley accused her of witchcraft and she was subjected to exorcism. The *Abbey Record* noted:

The Beast hearken to the Words of Alostrael His Concubine, perceiving clearly the Magical Need of making sure the circle against the Horror that had invaded it to such most cruel and deadly purpose; Wherefore with Wisdom of Tahuti did he conjure, exorcise and expel the aforesaid Ninette Fraux.

Crowley recorded the charge:

Ninette Fraux Do what thou wilt shall be the whole of the Law. Initiation purges. There is excreted a stench and a pestilence. In your case two have been killed outright, and the rest made ill. There are signs that the process may lead to purification and things made safe within a short time. But we cannot risk further damage; if the hate is still in course, it had better coil back on its source. Keep your diary going carefully. Go and live in Cefalu alone; go to the hospital alone; the day before you come out send up your diary, and I will reconsider things. I shall hope to see the ulcers healing. Do not answer this; simply do as I say. Love is the law, love under will.

In 1922, during a visit to London, Crowley met Frederick Charles Loveday (20), a graduate who took to calling himself Raoul. He had become a devotee of Crowley's works published in *The Equinox* while he was at Oxford. Alan Calder-Marshall was a fellow student and would recall Loveday as:

Loveday, when he was a scholar of St John's College, Oxford, was a stocky, untidy, carelessly dressed young man. Beneath his short hair, which was cut en brosse, having had a merry rather good-looking face, with bright blue eyes of incredible innocence. He was a good soccer player and a spectacular climber. After the college gates were closed at midnight, he regularly climbed in and out. His feat of climbing the Martyrs' Memorial and cementing an enamel chamber-pot to the top won him a romantic fame throughout the university.[3]

Crowley had mastered the art of being able to 'read' people. He would have read Loveday very quickly as a sensitive and easily led young man in search of a spiritual leader. He also had a way of 'knowing' when he encountered a user of recreational drugs; I guess it takes one to know one. Raoul was the sort of man who would be prime candidate prey for Crowley and his hypnotic ways. In fact, he would spend the next three days with Crowley getting high taking ether. Crowley and Loveday remained in contact, and after the short time he spent with Crowley, he had become

---

3. Calder-Marshall, Arthur, *The Magic of My Youth* (Hart-Davis, 1951)

obsessed with the teachings and aura of The Beast. In October 1922, Crowley was on his way to Cefalù when he stopped off at Rome. He had clearly been pondering the matter and required a secretary, so he wrote to Loveday inviting him and his wife, West End model Betty May,. to join him at the 'Abbey.'

Betty May (born Bessie Golding) was a real character and free spirit who had the *joie de vivre* that was the epitome of the era. Betty had risen from a humble background and followed a Bohemian career as a singer, dancer and model. She had worked in Paris where she fell in with a violent criminal gang known as the Apaches, who gave her the name of 'Tigre' or Tiger Woman. The name stuck; it suited her. She was a wonderfully formidable firebrand when she needed to be. In the early 1920s, she was working in West London as a professional model and had been employed for artworks by Augustus John and sculpture by Jacob Epstein. She had met Raoul Lovelady at the Harlequin Club in Soho. They fell in love and they married a few weeks later. Betty May was a strong woman and worldly wise, probably far more so than Raoul, and this is worth bearing in mind when you read her account of what happened at the 'Abbey'.

The couple had very little money and their fare was paid by an acquaintance of Crowley's, a magician and retired concert agent named Robinson Smith. This would mean the young couple could get out to Sicily but would not have the money to return until they started to earn money. They didn't think through the ramifications of what would happen if things went wrong. Loveday was blinded to anything other than taking up his position with Crowley, a man he had rapidly come to idolise. He was well and truly under Crowley's 'spell'.

Raoul dropped his academic career and proceeded to Cefalù. Betty didn't want to go; she had met Crowley before and did not trust him but she was not going to let her husband down. She could see what it meant to him and probably thought it could be a new adventure. While on their way to Sicily, the couple stopped in Paris where they visited Betty's friend Nina Hamnett who she had known in London. Nina would recall of Raoul:

He was very good-looking, but looked half dead … He was very much intrigued with Crowley's views on magic. He had been very ill the year before and had had a serious operation. I had heard that the climate at Cefalù was terrible; heat, mosquitoes, and very bad food. The magical training I already knew was very arduous. I urged them not to go. I succeeded in keeping them in Paris for two days longer than they intended, but they were determined to go and I was powerless to prevent them.[4]

The couple arrived in Sicily on Sunday, 26 November 1922. Betty's harrowing account of the horrific events that happened next would be published in the *Sunday Express* in March 1923:

We reached Cefalù – a tiny town of one narrow street and a few houses straggling up the hillside. Lovely, indeed, but desolate. No one met us. It was 8.00 pm on a Sunday evening, dark and cold. We inquired if anyone knew of Crowley. Conversation was difficult. Some of the Sicilians spoke a little bad American; and my husband spoke a little worse Italian. But the name Crowley acted like a charm. They all knew 'The Great Beast' as they call him and half a dozen set out to guide us.

It was a long dreary climb up a muddy, mountainous path; and our first glimpse of the 'abbey' did not dispel my forebodings. It loomed up suddenly before us, the white house gleaming eerily and faint in the moonlight, one mysterious, flickering light shining from a small window …

In the mornings I worked; and gradually I saw things that in the fatigue and excitement of arrival I had not noticed. Vile pictures, some hanging on the walls and others engraved on them, horrified me. Tea became an impossible meal for me, the conversation was too sickeningly bestial. Crowley is, I should think, sexually mad; he sees and talks of nothing else. Time after time I used to leave the table; generally I was fetched back. It was a dreadful ordeal: silence for lunch, filth for tea.

He [*Raoul*] was initiated but would never tell me anything about the ceremony. All I know is he wore gorgeous robes, that the ceremony

---

4. Hamnett, Nina, *The Laughing Torso* (Constable, 1932)

lasted eight hours, and that he was presented with a guinea book –
for which he was supposed to pay …

By this time Crowley never spoke to me; all my orders came from
Leah. At tea one afternoon Crowley was in a most peculiar mood,
irritable and uneasy. Suddenly he rose and said 'There is an evil spirit
in this room.' I felt annoyed 'Oh sit down man!' I said. He sat down,
and noticed a cat sitting by his seat – a lovely, tortoise-shell animal.
Crowley went to pick it up; the cat scratched him viciously on the
arm, and wriggled from his hands.

'Within three days' ordained the Beast 'that cat must be sacrificed.'
Then a remarkable thing happened. Crowley came into the kitchen
and saw the cat sitting by the window. As a rule, this cat would run
away if anyone came near it; but Crowley approached it, made passed
with his 'magic word' and the cat never moved. It was probably
hypnotism, but it was uncanny.

The third day arrived. I wanted to get the cat away, but my husband
told me not to interfere. But I took the animal a long way from the
house, and put it down, saying, childishly, perhaps 'Stay there pussy,
if you value your life.' But it followed me back.

Crowley had told my husband that he must kill the cat, and to
write out an invocation. Imagine the effect of such instructions on
a highly sensitive man like my husband. He went ashen pale and
trembling as he heard the words, but the Beast's influence over him
was such he could not refuse. He caught the cat and put it in a bag.
The animal cried pitifully.

The hour arrived. I refused, as always, to sit in the magic circle,
but insisted on being present. I took a seat close to the door, so that
I could escape if I wanted to. The altar was dressed for the occasion
with 'Cakes of Light.' It is impossible to describe of what these
were made. I do not believe any normal mind could ever imagine
the ingredients. Above the altar hung a bell, formed of an almost
flat metal disc, the striker being a human bone. A bowl to catch the
cat's blood stood at the side.

My husband trembling from head to foot, stood by the altar,
armed with a kukri – the sharp, carved sword that the Ghurka find
so effective. He had to lift the cat in one hand, and kill it with the

other. The cat struggled violently. Crowley dabbed its nose with ether till it became quiet enough to hold.

The reading on the long incantation concluded. 'Now,' said the Beast. My husband struck at the wretched cat, but his blow lacked force. He only half killed the poor animal, and dropped it. The cat, pouring blood from its throat, dashed away into Jane's room, leaving a red trail behind it.

Crowley ordered me to fetch it back. I refused, so he went himself. My unhappy husband was forced to pick it up again, and finally with another hard blow severed the cat's head from its body. The body fell to the floor with a thud that I can still hear.

Jane hid the body of the cat – which happened to belong to our nearest neighbour – and threw it in the sea the following day. Other incidents and practices indulged in at the 'abbey' it is impossible to describe. They are too terrible. With every day my horror and repulsion grew; my sense of foreboding, too, increased, but we could not get away. We had no money.[5]

In later published accounts, Betty would reveal that after killing the cat her husband had been commanded to drink some of its blood. As the days passed, Betty became increasingly dizzy and feverish until one day she could not work and collapsed. She asked for a doctor, was duly attended, received treatment and was recovering well when Raoul was seized by enteritis. Crowley initially refused to send for the doctor but eventually he must have relented as one did arrive. Sadly, Raoul continued to decline, he became very weak, often complaining of feeling cold, he had no energy and he could no longer write letters nor entries for his magical diary.

As he lay in his sick bed, Crowley decided Raoul's head should be shaved and set about doing so. As he shaved him, he inflicted a terrible cut to Raoul's head. His arms, too, were seen by Betty to be 'full of cuts'. This was because only Crowley could use the word 'I' while in the 'Abbey'; any initiate breaking that rule would have to inflict a cut on their arm.

Newspapers from England arrived at the 'Abbey' and Betty was about to read hers when Crowley entered the room and ordered, 'No papers to

---

5. *Sunday Express,* 4 March 1923

be read.' Betty retorted that she was going to read hers. Crowley stated he forbade it. Raoul intervened from his sick bed and told Crowley not to be a fool. Crowley snapped, 'I forbid it! If she reads her papers out of the 'abbey' she goes'. Betty went to read the paper and Crowley grabbed hold of her wrists, dragged her to the door and threw her out. As he did so, Betty threatened to go to the British Consul. Crowley just laughed then sneered: 'What can you do? Look at all my witnesses in the 'abbey' here – what is your word against theirs?'

It was late evening and dark by that time and Betty made her way to the village:

> I reached Cefalù as the townspeople were going home from their dance, it must have been a queer sight, the dancers in carnival costume, and myself in working clothes, my hair blown about by the wind, and my cheeks stained with tears.[6]

A local man she had occasionally seen at the 'Abbey' spotted her. He was concerned at the state she was in and came over. Betty told him what had happened. He suggested she should get a room at the hotel. Betty tearfully informed him that she had no money. He took her to the hotel and at the mention of the British Consul, she was given a room. The following morning, she wrote to the British consul at Palermo. Hardly had that letter left her when Jane Wolfe arrived with a note from Raoul. He was gravely ill. Betty was permitted to return to the 'abbey' to see Raoul. He was also attended by a local physician, Dr Maggio, who said he would send medicine but it came too late. Raoul died later that day, Friday, 16 February 1923.

Betty was permitted to see Raoul's body but she was not left alone with him. She, however, did see his body was covered with the punishment cuts. I cannot help but think back to the cat that Crowley had killed just to find out if cats really had nine lives. Or maybe he wanted to consecrate the soil of the land of his 'Abbey' at Cefalù with the burial of the first Thelemite to die in the Aeon of Horus, just as St Oran had died as a blood sacrifice so the land would be purified as Christian for St Columba on Iona. For Crowley, it was all about *his* will and *his* desires.

---

6. *Sunday Express*, 4 March 1923

Everything else was inconsequential to him, damn the consequences or who he damaged in the process.

The following day, Saturday, 17 February 1923, Raoul was transported to his place of burial on a finely decorated and draped hearse. Crowley donned his funeral robes and presided at the burial outside the cemetery in non-consecrated ground. The burial rites took the form of a Pentagram service and lasted an hour and a half. Loveday's parents later had his body exhumed and brought back to England for reburial.

Betty was only permitted to attend at her insistence. Betty had received money from the British Consul, and once the funeral was over, she had determined to get away. Betty recalled:

Escape – that was my one thought. Crowley, who had avoided me up to this, now came to me. 'You will make this your home,' he said. 'This is your life. You have no money.' 'I will go. I have money. The British Consul has sent me fifty lire.' I clutched the money, afraid of losing it … he retorted 'You will be back here in three months.'

Such is the astounding power of this dreadful person that even now, back in London, I feel uneasy at his words. But I would not let him see my feelings. 'I am going,' I repeated. He turned to Leah. 'Keep her here at any cost' he commanded. 'She is to stay Leah. I charge you!' I turned and dashed for the door. The Beast saw I was going, he laid one finger on his lips and said in a tone half of advice and half of menace: 'Silence, you understand.'

Betty met with the British Consul in Palermo, and with his generous help, she successfully made her escape back to England but it did not seem like she could truly escape Crowley or his acolyte's from the 'Abbey'. Shortly after her return to London, Betty was at the house of an acquaintance and saw Jane Wolfe was there:

She [*Jane*] has already come to London: what will be the next more of this emissary of the Beast? The sight of her frightened me. I have told my story to the Sunday Express. I hope the widespread publicity will act as a deterrent to Crowley and his friends, and as a safeguard to me.[7]

---

7. *Sunday Express*, 4 March 1923

Crowley's activities came to the notice of the Fascist government under Benito Mussolini and they would not be tolerated. Crowley was given a deportation notice and he left Sicily in April 1923. After a brief sojourn in Tunis, Crowley moved back to Paris and pursued more of his magickal rites, writing and debauchery. French authorities became increasingly uncomfortable with Crowley's behaviour and he was deported in December 1928, taking his new priestess, Nicaraguan Maria Teresa Sanchez (Maria Teresa Ferrari de Miramar) with him to England and the pair were married in August 1929.

Crowley, 'The Wickedest Man in the World', was back in London in 1929. His latest novel, *Moonchild* and *The Spirit of Solitude*, the first two volumes of his autobiography, were due for publication by the new esoteric publisher, Mandrake Press of 41 Museum Street, Bloomsbury. The recent stories from the 'Abbey' in the press had elevated Crowley to his apogee of notoriety and incredible stories were being attributed to The Beast and his dark occult powers. John Symonds would record one of the legendary incidents attributed to Crowley at the time in *The Great Beast*; it is a story that is still told at literary gatherings, in the bookshops of Cecil Court and the Charing Cross Road in London to this day:

> Crowley had now reached the height of his fame or, if you will, infamy. Like Julius Caesar, he was the husband to every woman and the wife to every man. The stories about him were legion. John Watkins, whose bookshop of occult and mystical works still flourishes off Charing Cross Road, once invited Crowley to demonstrate his magic.
>
> 'Close your eyes,' said the Beast.
>
> Mr Watkins did so. When he opened them a moment later, all his books had vanished from the shelves. [8]

It is this passage from Symond's biography of Crowley, however, that appears without further qualification of what was stated in the last two lines that is particularly intriguing, especially when it is considered what happened to Marie Fornario:

---

8. Symonds, John, *The Great Beast* (Rider, 1952)

It was said, with what truth I do not know, that when he entered the Cafe Royal, a silence fell upon everyone and none dared speak till the demon Crowley had sat down. His appearance, decidedly, provoked an attitude of awe: his bulk and cold, staring eyes set in his fat, feminine face; his shaved head, oddness of dress, strange rings on his fingers, his sweet, slightly nauseous smell, and, finally, that impalpable sense of a man which poets and occultists call aura – relentless, mocking, the aura of the Wanderer of the Waste and the Great Wild Beast. Among the Lamas of Tibet are those initiates who are said to have the power of hypnotizing and causing death from a distance.

Marie Fornario held seances and occult gatherings at her homes when she lived on Bushwood Road, where a neighbour claimed it seemed as if she had 'joined every spiritualistic and advanced religious society in London'[9] and her housekeeper Mrs Mabel Varney would speak of how Marie had carried on her seances, gatherings, healing work and astral travel when she was living on Mortlake Road. In 1929, Marie was active in her field and was having her articles published in *The Occult Review*. Marie was very much 'on the scene' and was moving in the same circles as Crowley, and in some of the esoteric circles where he wished he could be but had made himself unwelcome.

Had they met personally or did Marie believe they had met on the astral plane, or both? Crowley could 'read' those whom he thought might be susceptible to his hypnotic powers. Symonds wrote of Crowley, 'his head is completely shaved, so that the hypnotic effect of his dark, staring eyes is enhanced – eyes that are at once cold and burning with some unearthly passion'. In fact, Symonds was quite frank about the matter: 'It seems that Crowley could hypnotise people of the impressionable kind, especially those who were looking for a Master'.[10] Several of those who encountered Crowley witnessed him use abilities or experienced them first-hand and would mention them in articles and memoirs.[11]

Even after quite brief encounters, it was Crowley's eyes that remain etched into the memory of those who met him.

---

9. *Richmond Herald*, 30 November 1929
10. Symonds, John, *The Great Beast* (Rider, 1952)
11. Calder-Marshall, Arthur, *The Magic of My Youth* (Hart-Davis, 1951)

In 1937, occultist and surrealist painter, Ithell Colquhoun, saw and heard Crowley talking at Watkins bookshop. She would describe him as 'a squarely built man of medium height who appeared to be in his middle sixties. His skin was the colour and texture of parchment, and thinning grey hair was scraped across the crown of his head'. His glasses 'straddling his nose' were 'set in a long heavy face'. In fact, his 'features were in no way remarkabl..' Crowley looked so ordinary but it was his eyes that left a lasting impression. Even twenty years after seeing him, Crowley's eyes were still etched boldly in Ithell's memory when she wrote a chapter on Crowley in Cornwall for her book *The Living Stones: Crownwall* (1957):

> People seem to have been puzzled by his eyes and have variously described them as 'black,' 'brown', 'yellow', 'green' and 'the colour of horn!' To me they seemed none of these, but a transparent grey like water. My guess that they were the kind of eyes whose pupils dilates and contracts with unusual rapidity, so that the tone and colour of the cornea appears to change with changing conditions. These conditions may equally be psychological as well as physical, depending as much on mood as on the intensity of light. In some of Crowley's photographs the eyes look dark and opaque, in others clear.[12]

Despite her study and knowledge of the occult, I think Marie Fornario would have been an easy victim for Crowley. He may have been aware of her from the circles in which they moved. He would have 'read' her as a lonely spinster in need of a master and he would target her because she had money. He would not know how much, but after a few of his questions dropped into conversation, he soon would have got an idea that there were some funds there to be had and he would try to wheedle out them of her, just like he had done to others.

I firmly believe Marie was a truly kind soul who would believe there was some good in everyone. She would not have wanted to follow Crowley but I fear she could never have imagined anyone, no matter how bad, could be as devious as Crowley. If his target was 'unguarded', Crowley could get into their mind rather like a computer virus and, once in, would attack

---

12. Colquhoun, Ithell, *The Living Stones: Cornwall* (Owen, 1957)

the host he invaded just as insidiously. I think he got to Marie. Recall how Marie wrote to Mrs Varney warning her: 'Do not be surprised if you do not hear from me for a long time. I have a terrible healing case'.[13]

Marie had removed herself to the holy island of Iona, a place of peace, faith and white magic, a safe place from dark forces and attempted to cleanse herself. During her stay, the dark force continued to plague her and it took a visible physical toll upon her. She prepared herself and the rite well. She observed the stars and found just the right location. She fasted. I like to imagine she saw the Green Ray she had longed to see at dawn or sunset while on Iona. Feeling charged up by the power of the ray, then having cut the cross for protection in the soil of the island, pure and naked in the moonlight, she went into trance to rid herself of this evil curse once and for all. But just as her old friend Violet Firth had feared Marie had 'stopped out on the astral too long'. The bitter chill of that mid-winter night saturated her corporeal body and she died from exposure.

If Crowley had driven Marie Fornario to undertake those rites because he had used his hypnotic power upon her, he was responsible for her death. Scottish law is quite clear on the matter today, and would have been so at the time of Marie's death, and for almost a century before:

> Murder is constituted by any wilful act causing the destruction of life, whether intended to kill, or displaying such wicked recklessness as to imply a disposition depraved enough to be regardless of consequences.[14]

The problem in the prosecution of an individual for this crime, first and foremost, is detecting the person who has died had been driven to conduct certain actions that resulted in their death or committed suicide because of the actions of another. Then comes the problem of proving it to a degree sufficient to obtain a conviction in a court of law.

I realise some readers, quite rightly, will think that to murder by hypnotism, to drive someone to take their own life through fear of the black magic 'spell' or 'curse' that they believe had been laid upon them,

---

13. *Reynolds's Newspaper*, 1 December 1929
14. Macdonald, *Criminal Law of Scotland* (1948) and see Archibald Alison, *Principles of the Criminal Law of Scotland* (Edinburgh, 1832)

stretches the bounds of credulity. Having discussed the matter with lecturers in psychiatry and professionals working in the field today, I am assured such a thing is possible and does occur. One of them explained it in simple terms of the human mind being such a powerful thing that if an individual is sufficiently convinced something is real in their mind, to that person, it *is* real.

Mind-to-mind control is yet to be proven but the absolute *belief* in it certainly exists and some people believe they have experienced it, just like Marie Fornario did. Dracula author Bram Stoker was fascinated by the idea of it. He corresponded with Sir Oliver Lodge on the matter and even included a mind-to-mind duel with a fatal outcome in his last novel *The Lair of the White Worm* (1911). It was 'known' among students of the occult who applied for membership of the Golden Dawn or its offshoot, the Alpha et Omega, that some astral visitation of their mind by a senior member or members considering their application was part of the vetting process.

Sir Arthur Conan Doyle believed he had experienced an astral probing and corresponded on the subject with the likes of Sylvan Muldoon, author of *The Projection of the Astral Body* (1929). Doyle wrote in an article first published in *Pearson's Magazine* in April 1924 as 'What Comes After Death' and reprinted in October and December 1925 as 'Psychic Experiences':

> It is hard when a man has taught all his life that the brain governs spirit, to have to learn after all that it may be spirit which acts independently of the human brain. But it is their super-materialism which is the real difficulty with which we now have to contend.

In *My Religion* (1925), a number of popular writers expounded what they believed and Doyle was asked to be one of the contributors, taking the opportunity to explain further:

> Then came the strange experiences which slowly made me realise that rational agnosticism is not a terminus of our journey, but rather a junction where one changes from an old line on to a new one. My mind had hitherto been filled with an ignorant and unreasoning

contempt for psychic subjects. They ran clean counter to all my views, and seemed to me to be half fancy and half fraud.

But telepathy gave me pause. My whole previous case rested upon the supposition that brain produced soul or mind. But if the brain could indeed affect another brain at a distance, then, clearly, there was something there which was psychic rather than material. I made sure of telepathy by personal experiment. It shook the whole fabric of my philosophy and enlarged my ideas of the possible…[15]

Ithell Colquhoun described her experience of an astral probe of her mind after she applied to join the Alpha et Omega in her book *Sword of Wisdom: MacGregor Mathers and the Golden Dawn* (1975):

I felt a strange sensation as I was falling asleep. Long afterwards I used it as basis for a description in my Gothick novel, *Goose of Hermogenes* (1961), so I cannot do better than quote from this;

'… as though someone were exploring me, not physically but on some less palpable plane; or trying to influence me by acting directly upon my will without the normal media of words or other suggestions. Once, the impression of psychic attack or invasion was so strong I needed all my force to resist it. None the less, my will was instinctively set on resistance, since I felt that unless I succeeded in this I should be irretrievably swept away. A kind of paralysis descended on my limbs as I fought; and so much energy was drained from my physical form that I found myself for some while unable to stir.'

The only modification I would make to the above is to leave out the word 'attack' though I think it fair to retain 'invasion'. I felt neither fear nor hostility towards the influence, whatever it was – I suppose, because it was not antagonistic to me, only searching. It seemed impersonal: can I call it a grey influence? I had no impression of an

---

15. Doyle, Sir Arthur Conan, *My Religion* (Hutchinson, 1925)

individuality behind it though I do recall something like an 'interior' sound or distant vibration.[16]

In extreme cases, a strong belief or perception in a human mind can even manifest in physical symptoms such as a person who has come to believe he is a young First World War veteran (he was born decades after the Second World War) who had been in combat at the Battle of the Somme and physically manifests and suffers the effects of shell shock. Another example is the case of a woman who believes part of her body had caught fire, but is known not to have been exposed to flames of anything that could cause a burn of any kind, but is so utterly convinced of it, blisters erupt on her skin.

If Crowley could 'read' people as many believed he could, he could target his prey and given the right circumstances and a sufficiently receptive victim, he could rapidly effect his hypnotic powers upon them so they would either become his acolyte or be damned. A tragic example is that of Augusta Erskine in December 1934.

It was the year Crowley had been involved in a high-profile libel case in which he had taken Nina Hamnett to court for suggesting in her published memoirs *The Laughing Torso* that Crowley had practiced 'Black Magic'. The offending text stated:

> Crowley had a temple in Cefalu in Sicily. He was supposed to practise Black Magic there, and one day a baby was said to have disappeared mysteriously. There was also a goat there. This all pointed to Black Magic, so people said, and the inhabitants of the village were frightened of him ...[17]

Betty May came forward as a witness and gave testimony to foul treatment and the death of her husband Raoul Loveday and her own terrible experiences of Crowley at the 'Abbey' at Cefalù and it was widely reported in the press, as it had been in the *Sunday Express* shortly after the events happened over ten years earlier in 1923 – but Crowley had not sued back then! Crowley's solicitors could not find anyone who was prepared to stand

---

16. Colquhoun, Ithell, *Sword of Wisdom: MacGregor Mathers and the Golden Dawn* (Spearman, 1975)
17. Hamnett, Nina, *The Laughing Torso* (Constable, 1932)

up in court to enter the witness box to speak favourably of The Beast. J D Beresford did, however, write to Crowley suggesting it would probably be in Crowley's best interests to just drop the proceedings, pointing out:

> I haven't the least doubt that some very extraordinary and damaging charges will be made against you that would spoil any chance you might have with a judge, who is a kind of professional moralist.[18]

Crowley would not be dissuaded. The case heard testimony of Crowley's vile activities and his case collapsed. The judge, Mr Justice Swift, did not hold back his utter disgust of Crowley in his summing up:

> I have been over forty years engaged in the administration of the law in one capacity or another. I thought that I knew of every conceivable form of wickedness.
> I thought that everything which was vicious and bad had been produced at one time or another before me. I have learnt in this case that we can always learn something more if we live long enough.
> I have never heard such dreadful, horrible, blasphemous and abominable stuff as that which has been produced by the man who describes himself to you as the greatest living poet.[19]

Crowley launched an appeal that failed too and cost Crowley dearly in legal fees. By Christmas 1934, he was facing bankruptcy so it can easily be imagined just how desperate Crowley was at this time to find a suitable rich and vulnerable victim to fall prey to his hypnotic powers and resolve his financial woes.

Enter Miss Violet Marjorie Augusta Kennedy Erskine (37), known to her friends as Augusta, a wealthy spinster of a family connected with the House of Dun, Montrose, Scotland, for over 500 years. Miss Erskine had been staying at the exclusive Empress Club on Dover Street in Mayfair. The Empress was a women-only club with a room containing a bed and a bathroom for members wishing to stay. Guests were permitted but only in the members and guests' cloakroom, the lounge and the smoking gallery.

18. Symonds, John, *The Great Beast* (Rider, 1951)
19. *Daily Record,* Saturday 14 April 1934

Miss Erskine encountered a man in a hotel while she was in London who was described in the press as 'a dealer in Black magic'. As a result of the encounter, she was left believing he had a malevolent spell over her and it had begun to prey on her mind to such a degree she was unable to travel home for Christmas.

Augusta was found dead in her room at the hotel by one of the maids on 25 December, Christmas Day. PC William Littlejohn was called to the scene and stated at the inquest before the Westminster coroner, Mr Ingleby Oddie:

Miss Erskine was fully clothed except for the right stocking. Tied very tightly round the neck was a white scarf and stuffed into her mouth was a large piece of blue silk material. A great deal of this was hanging out of her mouth.

Dr John Taylor carried out the post-mortem examination and would state at the inquest that the scarf had caused a deep depression around the woman's neck and was so tightly tied that he could only just get his finger underneath it. He stated the cause of death as 'Congestion of the brain arising from asphyxia, strangulation and suffocation'.[20]

Augusta's mother, Mrs Alice Erskine, gave evidence that her daughter came to London from Huntingdon Park, Herefordshire, where she had been staying. The coroner asked after her daughter's general health and enquired if she had been sleeping well? Mrs Erskine confirmed that Augusta had suffered from a bout of the flu but had recovered, was in good health and had been sleeping well. The Coroner then asked:

Have you heard of any delusions that she suffered from?
To which Mrs Eskine replied firmly, 'Never, until this terror that she seems to have had the night before this happened.'
'What was that?' enquired the coroner.
'Well, I don't know', Mrs Erskine replied, appearing embarrassed
The coroner enquired, 'Didn't she have some kind of fear about some one getting an influence over her?'

---

20. *Daily Express*, Friday 28 December 1934

To which Mrs Erskine replied: 'She [Augusta] had a great dislike for anything pertaining to spiritualism or black magic or those sorts of things, and she did, I believe, meet someone. I do not wish to bring him in. I know nothing about him. She did think he dabbled in those things. A lot of people do. That frightened her.'

The coroner asked if her daughter had spoken to a young lady, a certain Miss Rumley. Mrs. Erskine confirmed that she had and added: 'She [Miss Rumley] did not like him. His atmosphere was not good.'[21]

Significantly, Miss Erskine had told Miss Rumley that she thought the Black Magician 'was getting an influence over her'.

The coroner recorded a verdict of 'Suicide while of unsound mind'.[22]

Having had a sheltered upbringing and a charmed life, Miss Erskine would have had no idea how to protect herself from Crowley's hypnotic powers. Her mother did not wish to be dragged into a potentially costly and embarrassing legal action like the 'Black Magic' case earlier that year. She would also have wanted to play down the tragedy because there was far more shame than sympathy attached to having someone commit suicide in your family, particularly in polite society in the 1920s. Not wishing to have her family name tarnished by any association with The Beast, I believe the man Mrs Alice Erskine refused to name in court was Aleister Crowley.

---

21. *Daily Express*, Friday 28 December 1934
22. *Manchester Evening News*, Thursday 27 December 1934

Chapter 13

The Curse of Crowley

Push imagination to the point of vision, and the trick is done.
William Blake

Over the years, newspapers have talked of the 'Curse of the Beast' or the 'Curse of Crowley' if some apparently paranormal activity takes place or there is an unexplained disastrous fire that sweeps through somewhere that Crowley used to live. The number of those who were close to Crowley who appear to have suffered misfortune or died painfully before their time could give one pause for thought if you are so inclined.

For want of a better place to start, **Samuel Liddell MacGregor Mathers** (1854–1918), one of the founders of the Hermetic Order of the Golden Dawn, which became one of the most influential organisations in the Western Mystery Tradition, and translator of the *Sacred Magic of Abramelin the Mage*. Mathers was also the man who initiated Crowley into the Golden Dawn but he dropped Mathers as one of his friends after he became convinced Mathers was working magic against him. Mathers died in November 1918 from the Spanish flu but Crowley was blamed for his death.

Frederick Charles 'Raoul' Loveday (1900–1923), a promising Oxford graduate, poet and initiate of Crowley. Loveday is believed to have died from enteritis caught from the unsanitary water at the 'Abbey' at Cefalù. He had also been ordered to drink cat's blood and eat the 'Cakes of Light' that were made from ingredients that 'no normal mind could ever imagine'. These abominations of Holy wafers were made of oatmeal, honey, red wine, animal or menstrual blood. Raoul was also weakened through the loss of blood from the numerous punishment cuts all over his body and probably suffered additional infections from the wounds or even tetanus. He would also have knowingly and unknowingly ingested a variety of drugs administered by Crowley while he was there. Raoul was initially denied medical treatment by Crowley and would only be attended by a doctor and receive the medicine he required when it was too late to save him. It could be suggested that Raoul was like the unfortunate cat of Crowley's youth and The Beast used him to explore how many ways he could kill a man before he finally died on 16 February 1923.

Theodore William Carte Moriarty (1873–1923), Hermetic Theosophist, Freemason, trance healer, teacher and the man who Dion Fortune based her lead character on for her *Dr Taverner* stories. Moriarty had his own mystical skills and wealthy sponsors. Crowley could easily have been jealous of such competition. Moriarty suddenly dropped dead at the Duke's Head Hotel, King's Lynn, Norfolk, on 18 August 1923. His cause of death was recorded as 'angina pectoris', a heart attack. In the occult world, the suspicion was that Moriarty had been killed by a 'psychic attack'. After Moriarty's death, Gwen Stafford-Allen attempted to continue the college at The Grange but Moriarty was irreplaceable. The Grange closed and was sold within a handful of years and Gwen Stafford Allen never embarked on another similar project.

Moina Mathers (1865–1928), artist and mystic. Born Mina Bergson, she was the wife of MacGregor Mathers and she carried on the Rosicrucian Order of Alpha et Omega as Imperatrix in London after her husband's death in 1918. In 1927, she started refusing to eat. She did not state the reason but some would wonder if she was starving to purify herself before undertaking a ritual. Some would suggest it had been her desire to die so that she could shed her physical body, perhaps to finally be rid of the dark entity that had entered it. Moina Mathers died on 25 July 1928 at St Mary Abbot's Hospital, Marloes Road, Kensington.

Maria Teresa de Miramar (1894–1955), Crowley's 'High Priestess of Voodoo' and his second wife. The pair married in August 1929 but Crowley soon tired of her. By 1932, he wanted to divorce her but was worried she was going to sue for a settlement from what money he had.

Then, as if by magic, Crowley's problem was solved when Maria Teresa was committed to Colney Hatch Lunatic Asylum (the same institution where Crowley had had his first wife committed). It was claimed Maria Teresa was suffering from delusions. The Medical Superintendent stated she believed herself to be 'the daughter of the King and Queen and that she had married her brother, the Prince of Wale..' She would remain in the institution until her death in 1955.

Norman Mudd (1899–1934), Oxford graduate and acolyte of Crowley. The death of Norman Mudd initially appears far from magickal. This tragic man with a weak personality had been mesmerised by Crowley from the moment they first met when Mudd was still a student at Trinity in 1907. He would become one of Crowley's most loyal followers. After Raoul Loveday died, Crowley required a replacement so he snapped his fingers (he actually sent a letter) and Mudd came running. At the time, Mudd had a good position as a lecturer in Applied Mathematics at Grey University College, Bloemfontein, South Africa. On receipt of the letter, as John Symonds put it so well in *The Beast*:

> he [*Mudd*] gave up his job, proceeded straight to Cefalu and saluted the Beast, his 'Lord and Master', with the enthusiasm of a man who thinks that he is at last really getting somewhere. He arrived on 22 April 1923, and handed Crowley his savings as a mark of respect and affection.[1]

Crowley used his loyal acolyte Mudd and his money as long as he was useful to him, then discarded him like a used rag. Crowley had prophesied, or would later claim to have prophesied, that Mudd would die by drowning, and so he did. On 16 June 1934, a body was recovered from Portelet Bay on the charming Channel Island island of Guernsey. It was fully clothed with cycle clips around the bottom of the trousers and all his pockets were filled with stones. Or at least that is what Crowley biographies tell you, but it was not quite so clear-cut.

Press reports reveal Mudd had been found in the bay 'standing upright with one arm over a mooring rope and with a tourniquet tightly bound

---

1. Symonds, John, *The Great Beast* (Rider, 1952)

round his neck'. Mudd had been staying alone at a local hotel and had been missing since the previous evening. The hotel porter identified the body as that of their missing guest. Newspaper accounts add a list was found in his room stating 'Equipment – Heavy boots, stick, script, cigarettes, trouser clips, stones and watch. All these articles were found on him'. There was no suicide note. The fact he took a script and a watch does leave one wondering if he was planning to carry out some rite rather than end it all. What was written in the script is not recorded.[2]

The home address Mudd had given when he booked in at the hotel was 220 Arlington Road, NW 1. Enquiries were made by the Metropolitan Police and the address was revealed to be a London County Council Common Lodging House. Police were unable to trace relatives or friends. An inquest was held on 18 June and a verdict of 'suicide' was returned. Norman Mudd MA was buried in plot No. 8, grave No.1 in the New Cemetery, Forest, Guernsey, on 20 June 1934.

Violet Marjorie Augusta Kennedy Erskine (1897–1932), eldest daughter of the noble House of Dun, Montrose, Scotland. This wealthy young lady had always rejected involvement in any part of the dark arts. She was also terrified by it. She encountered 'a dealer in Black Magic' at a London hotel. Convinced he had put an evil spell upon her, she committed suicide in her hotel room on Christmas Day, 1934.

Katherine 'Ka' Arnold-Forster (1887–1938), Fabian and Cambridge graduate, one-time lover of the poet Rupert Brooke, was one of the Neo-Pagans, a friend of Virginia Woolfe and was part of the Bloomsbury Group. Ka married Will Arnold-Forster in 1918. The couple moved to Cornwall and made their home at a house called Eagle's Nest near Zennor. Will became a Labour politician and Ka became the county's first woman magistrate. Mr and Mrs Arnold Forster were also instrumental in founding Gordonstoun School in Scotland in 1934.

A short distance away from Eagle's Nest was a cottage known as The Carn that had been occupied by a young couple Gerald Vaughan (23) and his wife Ellaline, affectionately known as 'Elfie' (24), and their infant

---

2. *Belfast News-Letter,* Tuesday 19 June 1934

son Patrick who had been born in December 1937. The Vaughans soon became friends with the Arnold-Forsters.

In the New Year of 1938, unexplained things began to happen around The Carn. Strange figures were seen silhouetted against the curtained windows of the cottage on moonlit nights. Piles of stones near the cottage would also mysteriously move overnight. Were the locals trying to frighten the Vaughans away for some reason? Ellaline had started to see and hear unexplained things. The question that remained unanswered was whether she was hallucinating, or was she seeing things that were more paranormal than just a trick of the mind? Gerald had heard some of the things that Ellaline heard too but he wanted someone else's opinion in addition to his own.

On Sunday 22 May 1938, Will Arnold-Forster was away on political business and the Vaughan's invited Ka over for dinner to see if she would see or hear what they had been experiencing. According to the Vaughans, Ka appeared to doze off after the meal and Gerald let her sleep. In the early hours of 23 May, he realised that she was not actually sleeping, and he feared that she had died. They called for the local doctor, who arrived promptly and sadly could only confirm that Ka was indeed dead. A post-mortem examination revealed Ka had died from a cerebral haemorrhage.

Paul Newman, the former editor of *Abraxas* magazine, uncovered a story that the Vaughans had been drawn into a black magic circle by Aleister Crowley. In this version of events, the Vaughans had become deeply concerned that a poltergeist or invisible demon that had been raised by their devil worship was now haunting their home. Worried that it may just be a trick of their minds, they invited Ka to join them on the night of 22 May to see if she would see or hear the same things that they did but Ka ended up dead. Mr Newman spent years researching the events of that night and the people involved. He published his findings in the *Tregarthen Horror* (Abraxas 2005) and in an article for *Fortean Times* (FT231) in February 2008.

Much of the latter story is dismissed by some who believe it stems solely from the novel *Talk of the Devil* by Frank Baker, published in 1956. The setting is Cornwall. Many of the place names are changed to centre around the areas of the fictional town of St Zenac but they are easily recognised by those who known them as in and around Zennor. In the book, one of his key characters is Nathaniel Sylvester, who is clearly based on Crowley.

Baker lived and worked in Cornwall as an organist for Bernard Walke at the church of St Hilary, Penwith. Baker skilfully evokes vivid images of the land and the magick rituals practiced there in his novel but they are, like the places he describes, not all complete figments of the author's imagination. Crowley had friends in the area in the late 1930s. He certainly met up with some of them on his visit but only named them by their initials in his diary. Those who lived in the area were also aware of stories of witches, ritualistic gatherings and witchcraft in the area in the 1930s. In fact, stories of communities immersed in witchcraft in Cornwall can be traced for centuries before and over the decades since.

These lingering stories and beliefs held by locals in the remote communities out in the wilds of Cornwall proved to be the inspiration for David Pinner to set his novel *Ritual* (1967). Pinner sets his story in the fictional rural village of Thorn, where a young girl appears to have been the victim of a ritual murder and a police detective from outside the area comes to investigate. In turn, *Ritual* provided the inspiration for the classic British folk horror film *The Wicker Man* (1973).

The composer and music critic, Cecil Gray, described the undercurrent of the occult that permeates Cornwall in his autobiography *Musical Chairs or Between Two Stools* (1948):

It is a magical place, but the magic is black … the north Atlantic coast … with its desolate moors strewn with Druidic monuments and fallen cromlechs and ancient abandoned tin mines … Altogether it is like entering the kind of country described by Algernon Blackwood or Arthur Machen – a land in which the boundary between the subjective and the objective becomes vague and indecisive. You begin to distrust the evidence of your senses, and to realise uneasily that things are not always what they seem to be, and this feeling becomes steadily intensified as you leave St Ives and – passing Tregerthen Farm and the cottage in which D. H. Lawrence lived during the years I knew him – approach the village of Zennor, where the innermost periphery of this spiritual Black Country begins.

Ithell Colquhoun noted some of the rumours and local stories in *The Living Stones: Cornwall* (1957):

> Folklore in Cornwall is not a thing of the past only but a living activity. Nor is it manifested only in more or less self-conscious revivals of ancient custom: where its remembrance has sunk below a subliminal level, it is still only just below. In the collective unconscious, the mythopoeic faculty is busy yet … if a 'black magician' had not been found in West Penwith fairly recently, somebody is sure to have invented one … the man whom the sensational press is still calling 'the wickedest man in the world' (though he died almost ten years ago) paid a visit to Mousehole. This was a gift to gossip which flourishes like an exotic plant in the soft moist air; from rumours still current in the neighbourhood, and even beyond.
>
> One would suppose that 'the Beast' as Aleister Crowley indiscreetly styled himself, had made on several occasions a protracted stay. The accusations range widely in seriousness; some surely assert that he was a bad influence on the district; others, that he and his followers danced naked round the stone circle at Tregeseal; yet others that he performed 'black magic' rites on the rocks about Trevellos; that he revived Druidic cults involving human sacrifice and that his disciples in the locality still resort to this practice, kidnapping women for the purpose (one or two mysteries of disappearance which the police failed to solve are 'explained' in this way.) Not a word of factual evidence is brought forward in substantiation; how far those who spread such scandal are sincere if deluded it is hard to say …[3]

At this point, it is worth mentioning Crowley noted in his diary that he stayed at the Lobster Pot in Mousehole in August 1938. Using it as a base, he noted he travelled the area meeting friends.

He may have visited and stayed on other occasions too; there are periods before and after when Crowley's diaries are far more patchy. However, the story that Crowley stayed at or lived in Carn Cottage, where Ka Arnold-Forster died, does not appear to be true. That said, there seemed

---

3. Colquhoun, Ithell, *The Living Stones: Cornwall* (Owen, 1957)

to have been a strong belief among those who lived in the area in the 1940s that Crowley had rented a cottage *somewhere* near Zennor at some time in the 1930s or 40s. BBC presenter Gerald Priestland, author of *Postscript: with love to Penwith* (1992), who had a great affection for the area told of a house in the Land's End region in which Crowley stayed that was occupied at a later date by two women, one of whom was found dead years later and the other gabbling something about the devil having appeared to her. The reviewer of Denys Val Baker's *Art Colony by the Sea* (1959) in the *West Briton and Cornwall Advertiser* who wrote under the initials JHM who, when trying to be dismissive of the brief mention of black magic rites having been conducted in the area in the 1930s, may have let out more than he intended when he wrote:

> Crowley is said to have visited West Penwith on many occasions to conduct black masses – bohemians, black magic and all – were practiced by only a few, hardly any of them resident artists and none connected to St Ives. Crowley's henchman in Cornwall died in 1935. I knew him quite well and once spent a Christmas Eve with him. The only Black Mass I can remember was completely spoilt when everyone present turned tail and ran in sheer panic.
>
> Crowley came down after the war with a green eyed girl whom I had briefly met in London, and it was rumoured that some intellectual half bakes were chalking pentagrams on the studio floor. But I would not consider any of this important or interesting enough to be mentioned at the beginning of a book on the art colony of St Ives.[4]

Victor 'Vickybird' Benjamin Neuberg (1883–1940) was a talented poet, free thinker and author. He edited *The Poet's Corner* column for the *Sunday Referee* and published the early works of Dylan Thomas and Pamela Hansford Johnson. When Neuburg died in 1940, Dylan Thomas paid him this tribute:

> Vicky encouraged me as no one else has done … He possessed many kinds of genius, and not the least was his genius for drawing

---

4. *West Briton and Cornwall Advertiser,* Thursday 27 August 1959

to himself, by his wisdom, graveness, great humour and innocence, a feeling of trust and love that won't ever be forgotten.

Neuberg had been a loyal and supportive acolyte and lover of Crowley but he would be haunted throughout his life by the suicide of his lover Ione de Forest, a death that may or may not have involved the magick of Crowley. Crowley would certainly claim this had been the case in his book *Magick in Theory and Practice* (1929). Neuberg would recall how, after they split up, Crowley had cursed him when he was unguarded: 'It was such a foul curse. He cursed me to die. Of all the most loathsome, obscene and painful diseases he could think of.'[5] Neuberg had the curse directed at him by The Beast with full ritual and consequently, he was convinced the curse had every chance of working on him.

Neuberg had contracted tuberculosis (TB) while he was still with Crowley. Neuberg's friend and biographer, Jean Overton-Fuller, suggested his TB had been caused as a result of one of Crowley's masochistic rites of initiation to a higher degree, which allegedly could only be successfully completed by sleeping naked for ten nights on the floor of Boleskine in a litter of gorse. Neuberg would recall it was the cold that was a far greater torment than the prickles of the gorse.[6]

You may wonder if Neuburg ever saw through Crowley; he certainly did not welcome mention of him in later years. Jean Overton-Fuller recalled a telling conversation she witnessed between Vittoria Cremers and Vicky:

Speaking with immense force, Cremers said, 'Crowley wasn't a magician, Victor.' It was the first time I had heard his name used in its proper form. 'He wasn't White. He wasn't Black. Half-way in everything Crowley. He had enough knowledge to raise a current he couldn't control. Couldn't get it up. Couldn't get it down. So it went round and round.' She made a circular motion with her hand over her abdominal region. 'It drove him mad. He wasn't a magician, he was a maniac!' At moments she slapped her knee or made lightning passes in the air with her hands which, though thin and bony, seemed animated by a power almost electrical. Vicky, flinching, murmured, 'I

5. Fuller, Jean Overton, *The Magical Dilemma of Victor Neuberg* (Revised Edition) (Mandrake, 1990)
6. Fuller, Jean Overton, *The Magical Dilemma of Victor Neuberg* (Revised Edition) (Mandrake, 1990)

know … I know … 'All those books!' she said. 'Pseudo-scientific piffle.' 'They took a long time to write,' he said, as though to moderate what she had said …[7]

Year after year tuberculosis steadily consumed Vicky, causing him to be racked with terrible pains in his chest and to suffer a persistent cough that produced gobbets of phlegm and blood. Vicky would eventually die on 31 May 1940 and the home he shared with his lover, Runia Tharp, at 84 Boundary Road, St John's Wood, London. Runia was at his bedside when he died. Cause of death was recorded as 'tubercular pneumonia, and chronic phthisis'.

Violet Mary Firth (Dion Fortune) (1890–1946), occultist, author, trance medium and co-founder of the Fraternity of Inner Light and a key figure in the revival of the Western Mystery Tradition. Historian Ronald Hutton described her as the 'foremost female figure'[8] of early twentieth-century British occultism. She had learned much from her magical mentor, Theodore Moriarty, and carried on a remarkable journey through the study, theory, practice and writing on the occult in her own right. Violet died of leukaemia at Middlesex Hospital in January 1946. Sadly, over the years that followed, her books and achievements were somewhat overshadowed by the infamy of the darker magick and publications of Crowley.

Many would write about their encounters with Crowley. Some would write about Crowley in his lifetime based on his reputation alone and more recently, there has been much spin put on his writings in attempts to redeem him and excuse his more vitriolic and frankly dangerous rites, which he describes in his writings as his malevolent sense of humour. Here is Crowley's philosophy in his own words. I leave you to form your own opinions:

To hell with Christianity, Rationalism, Buddhism, all the lumber of centuries. I bring you a positive and primaeval fact, Magic by name; and with this I will build me a new Heaven and a new Earth. I want

7. Fuller, Jean Overton, *The Magical Dilemma of Victor Neuberg* (Revised Edition) (Mandrake, 1990)
8. Hutton, Ronald, *The Triumph of the Moon: A History of Modern Pagan Witchcraft* (Oxford, 1999)

none of your faint approval or faint dispraise; I want blasphemy, murder, rape, revolution, anything, bad or good, but strong.

He would go further and proclaim:

I have exposed myself to every form of disease, accident, and violence. I have driven myself to delight in dirty and disgusting debauches, and to devour human excrements and human flesh. I have mastered every mode of my mind and made myself a mortality more severe than any other in the world. A thousand years from now the world will be sitting in the sunset of Crowlianity …

To Crowley, people were disposable, but then everything was secondary to Crowley, particularly women: 'Morally and mentally, women were for me beneath contempt', he wrote and added 'Intellectually of course, they did not exist'.

Alan Calder-Marshall recalled visiting Crowley in later life at a twee, rented cottage in Knockholt near Sevenoaks in Kent. Surrounded by the knick-knackery of horse brasses, copper warming pans, ships in bottles and cretonne-covered arm chairs, it was hardly the setting befitting 'The Great Beast'. The Crowley he met was a shadow of the man he had known, as John Redfern conveyed in his review of Calder-Marshall's book *The Magic of My Youth*:

The Beast's abdominal muscles were sagging worse than ever. The devil incarnate of his young dreams had collapsed into an old party with a cockney accent and a taste for brandy … between drinks, Crowley tried to hypnotise Calder-Marshall. But his eyes were weak and rheumy, reminding him of a torch whose battery is failing.[9]

Crowley bailed out of London during the Second World War and took up residence in Torquay, one of his old haunts over the years. In this wartime move, he first stayed at the Grand Hotel as he sought out a suitable property where he could create a 'New' Abbey of Thelema in

---

9. *Daily Express*, Saturday 3 November 1951

Britain. In 1941, Crowley wrote of his vision to Lady Frieda Harris, who was creating the artwork for Crowley's Thoth tarot card deck:

> The ultimate aim is to have quite populous Abbeys, with every type of talent represented, so that there will be a body of capable and intelligent people to rule the herd, and save the useful elements in our past civilization from being swamped by it.

All did not run well for The Beast. He took up residence at a house known as The Gardens on Middle Warberry Road, where he was caught showing a light during the black-out at 12.35 am on 23 January 1941 and was handed a summons to appear before the Magistrates. Appearing under his real name of Edward Alexander Crowley and stating his occupation as 'a poet', he pleaded mitigation, having 'been ill and was unable to supervise the black-out'. Crowley was fined £2[10] (about £87 today) but that would not be the end of the matter.

Beaches had been closed, defences were constructed, mines had been laid, and much of the coast had been a restricted area since the first invasion scares of 1940. In January 1941, there were still fears of a German invasion in the Spring; there had already been plenty of scares of signalling to the enemy by flashing lights to guide enemy bombers or passing signals to enemy agents. Local people who were aware of Crowley's reputation were already twitchy about him taking up residence in the town and word began to go around that he was a 'Fifth Columnist', a Nazi sympathiser who had been attempting to signal to the enemy when he got caught showing the light and it seems like word spread quickly.

Crowley thought he had found the ideal property called 'Moongates', which he described as 'a perfect place for an artist and sun-worshipper. The people are crazy in much the same way as I am' but crestfallen he would write 'They changed their minds about letting it, just as I was ready to sign on'.

Crowley was on the move again before the war was over. In 1944, he was staying at The Bell Inn in Aston Clinton in Buckinghamshire and would move once more to become a live-in resident in the now demolished

---

10. *Torquay Times, and South Devon Advertiser,* Friday 14 February 1941

Netherwood House, a private guest house at The Ridge in Hastings, before the year was out. Crowley would die there on 1 December 1947. He was not, as some accounts would have us believe, penniless, but he nearly was. When Crowley's Will was published in 1949, it revealed he had left the sum of £18 plus some property and effects.

Art historian and author, James Laver, recalled in his autobiographical memoir, *Museum Piece* (1964), how he had received a letter from Crowley telling him how much he enjoyed his book *Nostradamus, or The Future Foretold* (1942) and invited Laver to pay him a visit. Laver travelled to Netherwood and would chat to Crowley in his room, wondering, but did not ask if he had purposely chosen room number 13 for his abode. Crowley sat up on his divan bed with a small table in front of him and began by asking Laver about his interest in occultism. Laver replied that he thought Magick was summed up in Blake's phrase, 'Push imagination to the point of vision, and the trick is done'. Crowley's reply was telling:

> Ah, you realise that Magick is something we do to ourselves. It is more convenient to assume the objective existence of an angel who gives us new knowledge than to allege that our invocation has awakened a super-natural power in ourselves.[11]

A retrospective in the *Bexhill Observer* on the fiftieth anniversary of Crowley's death recalled how Miss Clarke, the eccentric manager and housekeeper of Netherwood, spoke of how Crowley, even in his declining years, possessed 'an aura of unutterable evil'. According to the feature, Crowley still exercised his diabolical powers, causing fellow residents to crawl along on all fours, bark, whine and scratch at doors at a whim.[12]

Promptly, at 2.30 pm on 5 December 1947, the funeral service for Aleister Crowley was commenced at Woodvale Crematorium, Brighton. It was far from a grand affair; no magickal robes were worn. Newspapers carrying the story noted: '… there were 20 mourners, including five women. Among them was a Mrs Hilda Johnson of Leicester, a pretty young woman, exquisitely dressed in a magnificent fur, who dashed

---

11. *Liverpool Daily Post*, 3 February 1964
12. *Bexhill Observer*, Friday 2 January 1997

forward to place a bunch of pink carnations on the coffin'[13] as it moved through the gates to the crematorium. Years later, the *Liverpool Echo* would claim Scotland Yard detectives attended Crowley's funeral 'so they could take note of the famous, titled and influential followers who attended'.[14] William Connor, the *Daily Mirror* columnist, who wrote under the name of 'Cassandra', was at the crematorium and evocatively recorded his observations in his inimitable style in the paper:

A raw, dank day, with the leaves wet and muddy on the ground. Five minutes before the appointed time I went inside the chapel – a cold, hostile place with a few memorial plaques screwed to the walls, and significant empty spaces left below them by thrifty relatives who think they may be needed later on. To my left were a youth and a girl, a good-looking young couple, who I judged to be Italian. To the right were about a dozen people – an odd mixture of crumpled raincoats, coughs, bright scarves, a lack of haircuts and the indefinable spoor of Charlotte Street and Soho.[15]

Extracts from Crowley's *Magick in Theory and Practice* were read, as were passages from *The Book of the Law*, there were collects from the Gnostic Mass, a hymn to Pan and an anthem. 'Cassandra' noted of the final moments:

A little woman [Patricia McAlpine, the mother of one of Crowley's children] scurried forward and threw a spray of roses on the coffin. The rollers moved. The little furnace doors opened and the coffin, slightly askew, began to push its way past the black velvet curtain covering the hole in the wall.'[16]

The service was denounced at a subsequent town council meeting where Councillor H J Robin, chairman of the committee for the crematorium, stated: 'We have taken steps to prevent such an incident happening again'.[17]

---

13. *Leicester Daily Mercury*, Saturday 06 December 1947
14. *Liverpool Echo*, Wednesday 10 August 1977
15. *Daily Mirror*, Tuesday 09 December 1947
16. *Daily Mirror*, Tuesday 09 December 1947
17. *Daily News*, Friday 02 April 1948

Chapter 14

Beyond the Grave

Those who foretold it are dead. Those who can stop it are in grave danger.
Nostradamus

Even after the death of Aleister Crowley in 1947, the stories still lingered of the 'curse' that seemed to afflict those who had been around him. The first occurred less than 24 hours after Crowley died when Dr William Brown Thomson (68) was found dead in his bath in his Mayfair flat.

The connection was instantly drawn in the press. The *Daily Express* carried the front-page story of 'Magician Put Curse on Him: Crowley's Doctor Dies':

For more than three years Dr Thomson was Crowley's physician. At first Crowley went to a West End chemist to get morphia tablets on Thomson's prescription. A year ago Crowley tried to get more than was prescribed. After that Dr Thomson always went to the chemist with him. Three months ago Crowley's morphia was stopped. He put a curse on the doctor. But Scotland Yard are sure that both men died from natural causes.[1]

James Laver recounted a version of a story in which Dr Thomson advised Crowley, 'I am going to cut off your heroin.' To which The Beast snarled 'If you do I shall die– and I shall take you with me.'[2]

Betty May had lost her husband because of Crowley and 'disappeared' for twenty years after testifying at *The Laughing Torso* libel trial. 'Found' again in a semi-basement bedsitter on Luton Road, Chatham, in February 1955, she chatted to a *Daily Express* reporter, sipping tea.

---

1. *Daily Express,* Thursday 4 December 1947
2. *Liverpool Daily Post,* Monday 3 February 1964

Described as 'Still vivacious, still audacious, owning to 60 years, but looking little more than 40'. According to the report, Betty had 'headed North' after the trial and then camped out in a beauty spot for three years after the war, then took the bedsit. Betty had published her autobiography in 1929 and was found again after her publishers appealed for news of her. She said to the reporter after all she had been through, 'Won't it be fun if my publishers have accumulated some royalties for me?'[3] Betty May lived her latter years in Strood in Kent and died from a heart attack at Medway Maritime Hospital in Gillingham on 5 May 1980, aged 85.

Nina Hamnett, the talented artist and sculptress who had been a friend of Ione de Forest and gave evidence at her inquest, only for Crowley to claim his magic had caused Ione to commit suicide in his book *Magick in Theory and Practice* (1929). In her day, Augustus John had described Hamnett as one of the four best women painters. Nina Hamnett was also the author of *The Laughing Torso*, the book that Crowley sued for libel and was bankrupted by the loss of the case. In later life, Nina was the subject of retrospectives and magazine features in which she was heralded as 'Queen of Bohemia'. On Thursday, 13 December 1956, in a scene akin to something out of the film *The Omen*, Nina mysteriously fell out of a window of her flat in Westbourne Terrace, Paddington and smashed onto the pavement forty feet below. In one particularly gruesome newspaper report, it even claimed Nina had not only fallen but had ended up being impaled on the spikes of railings instead of the pavement.

Nina died a few days later from the injuries she had sustained in Paddington General Hospital on 16 December 1956. The last words she uttered were a plaintive cry of: 'Why don't they let me die?' At the inquest held at St. Pancras, the Coroner, Mr W. Bentley-Purchase, expressed his view, 'I think she was looking out of the window, overbalanced and was gone.' Satisfied there was no possibility of suicide, a verdict of 'accidental death' was recorded.[4]

Just four years later, retired Major Edward Grant, the then owner of Boleskine House, Crowley's Scottish home he bought specifically for the

---

3. *Daily Express*, Monday 14 February 1944
4. *Marylebone Mercury*, Friday 28 December 1956

performance of the Abramelin ritual, appeared to have been doomed. Grant suffered the misfortune of having his car mysteriously veer off the road and plunge down a 20ft embankment at Borlum, Fort Augustus, at the south end of Loch Ness in July 1960.[5] Given assistance by the occupants of a passing car, Major Grant was removed to Raigmore Hospital, Inverness, where he appeared to make a recovery. Four months later, Major Grant blew his head off with a shotgun in Crowley's old bedroom on the afternoon of Tuesday, 8 November 1960. Foul play was not suspected; he left no note and no apparent reason was suggested for his actions.[6]

Boleskine House was subsequently owned by Led Zeppelin guitarist Jimmy Page, who had become fascinated by Crowley and his works. Page sold the property in 1992 and the building suffered significant fire damage in December 2015 and again in July 2019. The building and its location are ideal for property investors but many of those who know it and its past would not consider purchasing it. For some, these events were quite enough. The curse of Crowley was carrying on beyond the grave.

At 2.30 pm on the afternoon of Wednesday, 16 March 1988, the body of a young woman was discovered by a member of the public in a rhododendron plantation in the Botany Bay area near Virginia Water at the southern edge of Windsor Great Park. She had long dark hair that was nearly waist length, which she had been wearing in a single plait tied up with a red silk ribbon. Her body was lying on what was described as 'a curtain' and was in an advanced stage of rigour mortis; in fact, she had been there for some months, and part of her face had been eaten away by insects.

The police began house-to-house enquiries and issued a description of the woman, who they believed to be aged between 18 and 23. She weighed 11st 7lbs and stood 5ft 3inches tall, 'was clean and well dressed and had the appearance of being an intellectual'. She was found wearing a mauve button-up shirt, pale blue jeans with a black plastic belt with a brass buckle. She also wore white canvas shoes and a black motorcycle jacket. The only belongings found with her were a Yale-type key on a blue plastic key ring that resembled a curly telephone flex and she was

---

5. *Inverness Courie,r* Friday 15 July 1960
6. *The Scotsman,* Wednesday 9 November 1960

wearing a red plastic Swatch watch that had points of the compass on it instead of numbers. She had no handbag or anything that might have identified her. Even pills and their containers found nearby gave no clues as to which chemist they came from. A post-mortem revealed she had died from an overdose of sleeping pills.

Only after months of enquiries and appeals drawing a blank did the police reveal to the public 'an odd assortment of items' including a bottle of Lucozade, candles, a packet of biscuits, and the book *Commentaries of AL* (*The Equinox* Vol. 5 No. 1) by Aleister Crowley had been found near the soaking wet body. She was eventually identified through the missing persons register as Miss Paula Carol Dean (31), who had lived with her parents in the Twickenham area.

The discovery of the Crowley book, candles or the circumstances of how she was found did not receive any particular mention in the newspaper reports of the inquest. The coroner recorded a verdict of 'death by suicide'.[7] Deaths associated with Crowley and his works are still occurring. The author is aware of some in more recent times but he does not mention them so as not to cause distress to recently bereaved families.

Over the decades since his death, there have been numerous individuals who claim to have followed Crowley's teachings laid out in his books and have harmed themselves and killed men, women and children in the name of Aleister Crowley or his rituals. There are also those who have lost their lives trying to protect themselves or have even been driven to commit suicide to escape from the curses they believe have been placed upon them by those working Crowley's magick.

In ending this book, I could do no better than commend you, dear readers, to seriously consider Dennis Wheatley's salutary warning in the introduction to his novel *The Devil Rides Out*:

Should any of my readers incline to a serious study of the subject and thus come into contact with a man or woman of Power, I feel that it is only right to urge them, most strongly, to refrain from being drawn into the practice of the Secret Art in any way. My own

---

7. *Staines & Egham News*, Thursday 15 September 1988

observations have led me to an absolute conviction that to do so
would bring them into dangers of a very real and concrete nature.[8]
To all of you, especially those who tread the paths of research into dark
history and the paranormal, I say, please be kind to each other and let's
be careful out there.

---

8. Wheatley, Dennis *The Devil Rides Out* (Hutchinson 1934)

Appendix 1

"*Myths of the Norse*" The Lost First Lecture of Miss Marie Fornario presented to the Bishop's Stortford Students' Association at the Technical Institute on the evening of Monday, 21 February 1921

Sadly, Marie does not appear to have written up the research for her lecture into a published paper. At least no copy of it has been found to date, but fortunately, an account of her lecture was published in the *Herts and Essex Observer* on Saturday,, 26 February 1921, so we can gain some idea of its tenor and scope:

An interesting address on "Myths of the Norse" was given by Miss Fornario, who remarked that the ancient religion of the Norse should have an especial interest for them, partly because through it they could learn to understand something of their forefathers and partly because many traces of it had become part of everyday life, Tuesday, Wednesday, Thursday and Friday being named after Scandinavian divinities.

A sudden flood on the river Trent was also known as the "Aeger," the name of the old Norse sea god. Many of the exploits of Thor, the thunder god, had come down to them in the tales of "Jack the Giant-Killer." The chief god, Odin, represented the cloudy sky; he was the father of Balder, the sun-god, who was slain in ignorance by his blind brother, Winter; but Winter himself was slain by another son of Odin, who represented the returning Spring. The key-note of the old Norse faith was the deification of valour, as they believed that Odin had no use for cowards. When the Norseman were hopelessly cornered they fought to their last breath and then died cheerfully, rejoicing in the knowledge that they would have the company of many slain foes on their way to Odin's Hall, where they would all live happily. feasting and fighting till the last battle.

Their ancestors believed that earth, sea and sky were made from the flesh, blood and skull of a forest giant slain by the gods; while the clouds were thought to be his brains. Between the gods and the giants an eternal feud was can led on until the last battle of Ragnarok, at the end of the world, when, with the exception of three or four surviving deities, the opposing forces exterminated each other. The world was set on fire by the flame giants, and then drowned in the sea. But a long time afterwards the purified earth reappeared from the water, green and beautiful, and life commenced anew.

On the proposal of the President [Dr Young], a cordial vote of thanks was passed to the Lecturer.

Appendix 2

'The Immortal Hour, An Interpretation of the Play' by Fiona Macleod
By Mac Tyler, January 1923 (Frederick Newman, London 1923)

During the course of some three and twenty performances of *"The Immortal Hour,"* the writer of this booklet has gained much amusement from the comments of the audience, yet, if various remarks overheard on such occasions have enlivened the interval between the two acts with flashes of humour, (mostly unconscious on the part of the speakers), they also provided matter for considerable reflection.

Visitors to the Regent Theatre may be roughly classified as follows; students of mysticism and folk-lore who are able to understand the great truths concealed behind this gossamer curtain of faery; (a small clan, but they come frequently and every time discover some new aspect of illuminating significance), a large number of people who think the play beautiful but sad; and many for whom the whole drama is so elusive and incomprehensible that they irritably demand of each other "what on earth the fellow can be getting at," and are frankly bored: and there is a fourth class who, while keenly appreciating the artistic beauty of the performance, also sense the existence of a deeper meaning, but are hopelessly baffled by their inability to interpret the intricate symbolism employed.

It was for such seekers that this interpretation was written, and in the hope that these tentative suggestions, based on a study of comparative religion, folklore, mysticism and symbolism will provide them with the necessary clues.

While this Celtic allegory may be interpreted to represent the return of Spring to the world from the enforced thraldom of Winter, it will be apparent to all students of esoteric cults that we have here a drama similar to those employed in the ancient mysteries, and that the reactions and interaction of Dalua, Etain, Eochaid, Midir and the two peasants, symbolise the psychological and spiritual effects of initiation.

Practically all the religious systems of the ancient world, and most of the modern ones also, include two strongly differentiated types of teaching, the one exoteric, the other esoteric.

The exoteric or public side of any faith dealt with the moral precepts and ordinary religious ceremonies generally in use; the great truths underlying all religion were therein allegorised for the benefit of those who were not sufficiently evolved to grasp the fundamental philosophical concepts in their abstract form, and therefore had to be taught in terms of concrete things which are known to all.

The esoteric side dealt with the abstract philosophical concepts veiled by the exoteric symbolism. These ideas were never publicly proclaimed, but they were taught in secret all down the ages to such advanced individuals as were capable of understanding them, and who having reached a certain standard of moral, intellectual and spiritual development, were permitted to take part in the mysteries where they were instructed in the spiritual science of raising the lower self or personality to the level of the higher self or Individuality.

The allegories employed in the various exoteric systems seem to contradict each other but the esoteric interpretations are the same in every case, notwithstanding the apparent diversity of the different symbolism.

The Celtic mysteries are denoted by two mythological traditions; one is the Feast of Age, instituted by Manannan Mac Lir; the other is the Shadowy Fount of Beauty wherein the Salmon of Knowledge swims among berries fallen from the rowan, quicken tree or mountain ash, the Tree of Life in Celtic mythology, corresponding to Yggdrasil, the World Ash of the Scandinavians.

The opening speeches of the first scene of *"The Immortal Hour"* appertain to the world of thought; the stage is almost in darkness, vague shadows appear and disappear, denoting half-formulated concrete ideas strange and alien to Dalua, (who represents the abstract mentation of man), as that abstract mentation is itself alien to the emotions of normal humanity. The abstract mentation holds converse with half-caught intuitions which inform it that though it has travelled from one darkness to another, yet it has come:

"no further than a rood,
A little rood of ground in a circle woven,"

All this first scene is tremendously significant, a clue to much that follows afterwards, and that would be otherwise be incomprehensible. The working of the principal of polarity is clearly shown in Dalua's assertion that he is

"… not first or last of the Immortal clan
For whom the long ways of the world are brief
And the short ways heavy with unimagined time,"

Implying that the conditions of the physical world are reversed in the metaphysical.

Dalua, (who represents the abstract mentation of man), is recognised by the light of the wandering star above him, and the intuitions hail him, half mockingly, half fearfully,

"…Sad Shadows of pale hopes,
Forgotten dreams, madness of men's minds;
Outcast among the Gods, and called the Fool,
Yet dreaded even by those immortal eyes."

The Gods symbolise the highest type of emotional forces, but even these shrink from the cold impersonal detachment of the abstract mind, whose touch also wrecks the concrete mind if the latter has not been rendered sufficiently plastic by training to endure the shock of such an impact.

The chorus of intuitions now gives place to a chorus of demons symbolising the dark atavism of the subconscious forces which endeavour to acclaim the abstract mentation as part of their own evil, because the reaction of the lower principles to the mistranslated stimulus of the super-conscious frequently produces disastrous results on the material and lower emotional planes. This is why Dalua is said to bring madness and death, which generally result from misapplication of metaphysical forces.

In a marvellously orchestrated chorus of mocking laughter the demons gibe at the dreaded power who has unwittingly strayed among them. Dalua silences them with an angry gesture, bidding them laugh not,

> *"For Lu and Oengus laugh not, nor the gods*
> *Safe set above the perishable stars."*

The music here explains much that is left otherwise unexpressed. In the well-night perfect beauty of the Dalua motive we have all the sadness of mortal struggle and spiritual triumph marvellously interwoven, as in one flash of supreme vision the mind visualises its own high origin and lofty destiny, and unflinchingly carries out the plans of the forces whose tool it knows itself to be. It accepts the hatred and fear of the lower principles, which are unconscious of the law with which it co-operates, and, in realisation of the sublime ultimate purpose, it has already attained in essence, even though suffering in its own application of the law to itself and others.

Dalua is a composite figure, including many of the characteristics of Lucifer, Saturn and Pan. As Lucifer he tempts Etain, even as the serpent tempted Eve, and with a similar object; as Saturn he initiates Eochaid, weighing him in the balance and warning him that those led by dreams shall be misled, for those who seek initiation guided only by emotion and not by reason, cannot pass the necessary tests. Like Pan, who brought madness and death on those who confronted him unexpectedly, at the close of the play the Fairy Fool bestows the boon of death on the heart-broken king who demands from him the restoration of his dreams. The shadow of Dalua's hand, as applied to Etain and Eochaid to bring forgetfulness, corresponds to the draught of Lethe offered to souls about to descend into incarnation. It polarises their respective attitudes; Etain is made to forget her fairy kindred and high estate; Eochaid, who symbolises the desire principle, is made to imagine himself greater than he really is, a king of dreams and shadows, instead of their plaything, and a fit mate for the immortal Star of the Shee. The Shee are the Celtic gods, the spiritual emotions of man, which appear cold and cruelly callous to the warm passions of humanity.

Etain's appearance on the stage is marked by a slight increase of light, and as she represents the soul, we may surmise that this section of the play deals with the forces of the lower emotional or desire plane; the actual change from the mental plane to the desire takes place previous to this point and is denoted by the departure of the intuitions and the entrance of the demon chorus.

Etain is half fascinated, half terrified by Dalua, who suddenly during their conversation realises why their meeting in that strange place has been ordained, and tells her of the King of Men, who has wooed the Immortal Hour, and

> *"…sought and found and called upon the Shee*
> *To lead his love to one more beautiful*
> *Than any mortal main …*

But concludes sternly that there is only

> *"One way to that gate: it is not Love*
> *Aflame with all desire: but Love at peace."*

He then makes a significant gesture which is repeated at Eochaid's death. This gives us a very important clue to the cause of the tragedy. Eochaid's desire for initiation is prompted by a selfish longing to grasp and hold for himself something beyond the ordinary quality of joy, not by a desire for service, and because the motive of his quest is purely selfish, the hidden god speaking from the fountain warns him to return, but the warning is unheeded as Dalua's mocking laughter lures the king onward to his doom.

The second scene shows Etain sheltering from a storm in the hut of two peasants who represent animal instincts, and who are terrified both of her and of Eochaid, who seeks shelter from them also. The lower instincts are as much afraid of the desire principle, when that is seeking its higher self, as they are of the Soul, knowing full well that such an attempt towards unification, if successful, will inevitably be followed by an attempt at their own extinction. In this case it is not successful, as when they intreat Eochaid to do them no ill, he gives perfunctory assurances of his harmlessness towards them, while the rising tide of the great love duet surging in the orchestra denotes that he is hardly conscious of what he is saying, or of anything in all the world but the beauty of Etain.

She is equally swayed by emotion and moves towards him like one entranced, though when he kisses her hand, she breaks away, half conscious that she is transgressing. But the spell is too much for her; she yields to his passion and the love music reaches an ecstatic climax as they both sing

> *"The years, the bitter years of all the world*
> *Are now no more,"*

When the mockery of Dalua is heard from the orchestra, and Eochaid demands, half in anger, half in fear,

> *"Who laughed? What means that laughter?"*

Etain wearily seats herself at the other side of the stage, the king kneels by her side, and the two peasants slumber by the glowing fire, when suddenly a sound of far-away music is heard, and Etain rouses herself to listen to the song of the Shee. Eochaid hears nothing, and is both puzzled and troubled as she turns from him, and rises from her seat, with outstretched arms, straining towards the distant voices. She has remembered something of her true nature and passionately regrets her self-determined exile.

The scene of the second act is laid in Eochaid's dun, and shows us the rejoicing at the first anniversary of his wedding. After a chorus of bards and soldiers, Etain enters with her women, pale and sorrowful. During the first act, she wears the green gown of the fairy folk but now she is robed in gold and red; Eochaid who enters shortly afterwards is also robed in the red that symbolises passion, though in the first act he wears blue, the colour of aspiration.

Etain complains of weariness and announces her intention to retire, but Eochaid entreats her not to leave him, confessing that in spite of all the rejoicing he is *"sore wrought by dreams and premonitions,"* expressed by a sinister little chromatic passage in the orchestra. He has heard again the laughter of Dalua and senses the approach of trouble, but notwithstanding his request, Etain passes out with her women, and he dismisses the rest

of the court with the exception of an old bard and a page. The last two
Druids on the point of departure are startled by the sudden appearance
of a stranger in green, who stands in the doorway and hails the king,
apologising for his late appearance and requesting a boon. Eochaid is
somewhat disconcerted, but replies with dignity that

> *"… no stranger claims a boon in vain*
> *… if that boon be*
> *Such as I may grant without loss of fame*
> *Honour or common weal,"*

And enquires the name of the mysterious visitor. This the stranger refuses
to give but proclaims his royal lineage in a passage of exquisite beauty:

> *"I am a King's first son.*
> *My kingdom lies beyond your lordly realms*
> *O King, and yet upon our mist white shores*
> *The Three Great Waves of Eire rise in foam.*
> *But I am under sacred bonds*
> *To tell no man, not even the king,*
> *My name and lineage.*
> *King, I wish you well,*
> *Lordship and lands and all your heart's desire."*

Eochaid turns to him impulsively, then recollecting the presence of the
two Druids, he dismisses them, before confessing his longing

> *"To know there is no twilight hour*
> *Upon my day of joy;"*

The stranger reminds him that great poets have sung how

> *"Great love survives the night and climbs the stars,*
> *And lives the Immortal Hour along the brow,*
> *Of that Infinitude called Youth whom men*
> *Name Onegus Sunrise."*

But Eochaid is also a poet and desires a more definite reassurance. The stranger, who is Midir, a prince of the Fairy people, husband of Etain, and symbolises the Spirit, now leaves the entrance and comes forward, flinging wide his cloak, as if announcing himself the messenger of the gods. He sings of the Immortal Hour from a Cosmic standpoint, as exemplified by Aed and Dana, suggesting the immortality of love and its Cosmic significance, but Eochaid's reaction to this clarion challenge is in terms of personality, a passionate prayer that he and he alone may keep Etain forever, and so he misses his great opportunity.

Midir turns significantly away. Eochaid murmurs bitterly, *"Dreams, dreams,"* and then enquires what boon is desired by his visitor. He is still more troubled when Midir asks to touch the white hand of the queen, and to sing her a song, but the king has given his word, so he sends the page to summon her, and while they await her appearance, the old bard gives definite form in the following words to the vague uneasiness pervading the whole of this scene.

> *"I have seen all things pass and all things go*
> *Under the shadow of the drifting leaf;*
> *Green leaf, red leaf, brown leaf;*
> *Grey leaf blown to and fro,*
> *Blown to and fro.*
>
> *I have seen happy dreams rise up and pass*
> *Silent and swift as shadows on the grass*
> *Grey shadows of old dreams,*
> *Grey beauty of old dreams,*
> *Grey shadows on the grass."*

The old bard slowly hobbles away, and Etain enters, clad in the green robes of the first act. She starts when Eochaid speaks to her, and complains that she could not sleep, for her dreams came close and whispered in her ears. Eochaid informs her why he has summoned her, and Midir moves from behind a pillar into her line of vision. She looks at him in bewilderment, and when he kisses her hand she starts again, as though half remembering, then recovering herself, she prays him to sing his song, and he obeys in the words and melody used by the fairy people at the close of the first act. As the notes die away she stammers confusedly,

> *"I have heard, I have dreamed that song"*

In the next lyric Midir declares his identity; she rushes impulsively towards him, and then draws back, confused, as she remembers her desertion of him and her own unworthiness, but still he woos her with outstretched arms, and at length she comes to him, saying,

> *"I am a small green leaf in a great wood,*
> *And you are the wind o' the south."*

It is significant that after kissing Etain's hand, Midir carefully refrains from touching her again, even after her surrender, implying that though the spirit may descend to woo the soul and reclaim her, it is on alien ground in the lower planes, and their true relation cannot be resumed until the soul returns to the higher level.

Eochaid here endeavours to come between them but is repulsed by a gesture from Midir, who slowly moves backwards to the entrance, drawing Etain after him. She moves as though in a trance, and to Eochaid's passionate appeals she only replies gently,

> *"I cannot hear your words so far away,*
> *I go from dark to light*
> *and so passes out of his life, to the sound of the fairy chorus in the distance".*

This is the part most generally misunderstood, as the majority of people sympathise with Eochaid and feel that Etain has treated him badly.

The real clue to the situation lies in the fact that Eochaid and Midir are polarity aspects of the same principle; and therefore a unity. When Eochaid was offered his heart's desire, he could have gained the right to follow Etain to her immortal home, had he been content to sacrifice himself for her welfare, but because his love is selfish, he loses her objectively, and, though erroneously, feels that he has lost her irrevocably. If the lower nature is content to follow where the higher principles lead, it can be regenerated without suffering much of the pain entailed by its endeavour to drag down the soul; but a refusal to be regenerated necessitates its sacrifice that the soul may be liberated. Yet the lower nature and the higher are one in essence, though manifesting in opposite directions; and the death of Eochaid symbolises the metaphysical attainment of his heart's desire, since in the supreme surrender Love is at peace, as Dalua's gesture signifies, and this is the essential condition announced in the first act for all who would stand beside

> *"The rainbow gate of her whom none may find,*
> *The Beauty of all Beauty."*

The essence of Eochaid, all of him that is pure and great, (being almost the highest possible expression of the personality, truly a King of men,) is incorporated with the polarity aspect, Midir, and thus in the metaphysical world Midir-Eochaid hold Etain forever, and the cycle is complete. In the original play, Eochaid's entreaty to Dalua,

> *"My dreams, my dreams, give me my dreams,"*
> *is answered by the significant words,*
> *"There is no dream save this, the dream of death."*

Implying that death itself is only a dream and that the ultimate reality for Eochaid, as for Midir and Etain, lies in the other world, where all life is one Life.

This is not obvious to the majority of people, and it is unfortunate that this pregnant sentence was omitted; but the wonderful music of the closing bars, based on a re-statement of the Dalua theme, explains it with extraordinary clarity for those who can understand, and one watches the descent of the curtain convinced that in spite of the apparent tragedy, and notwithstanding struggle, illusion and mistakes, the end is peace and fulfilment for all.

The Immortal Hour was given only a few performances, the politics of its composer became an issue and it has disappeared from the theatre. But the music has lived on in recordings, the most famous being the lovely aria, *'The Lordly Ones'*.

"How beautiful they are the Lordly Ones
who dwell in the hills, in the Hollow Hills.
They have faces like flowers and their breath
is a wind that blows o'er sunny meadows
filled with dewy clover..."

Appendix 3

Report of the lecture '*An Account of Some Occult Experiences*' presented by Violet Firth for the Fellowship Club at 52, Lancaster Gate on the evening of Wednesday, 25 March 1925, published in the *Bayswater Chronicle*, 28 March 1925

Most of us at the present time are ever ready to welcome new ideas, new school of thought. The strenuosity of modern life demands it. We must have some centre where, forgetting the whirl and turmoil of present-day existence, we can quietly foregather, either for pleasant social intercourse or for the discussion of those more urgent and compelling problems of life itself.

Such a very obvious need is supplied by the Fellowship Club, 52, Lancaster Gate, where for a very modest annual subscription one can become a member of the Club, and be initiated into the 'mysteries' of the very latest modern school of thought, comprising such world-wide subjects as Theosophy Occultism, Healing and Meditation, Philosophy, together with the enjoyment of many delightful musical and dramatic recitals at frequent intervals.

Therefore, it was a large and interested audience which gathered in the handsomely decorated drawing room of the Club on Tuesday evening to hear Miss Violet Firth give her most interesting 'Account of some occult experiences.'

The lecturer, fair and exceedingly handsome and a true daughter of Yorkshire, said she was born in the particular part of that county which had been invaded by the Vikings of old. These ancient people were well known to possess certain occult powers. She owed her first occult experience to the fact that she was born in a haunted house. The 'ghost' was a very substantial one, and "bumped " about the house, dropping things on the floor and making a tremendous noise as he came and went. But she contrived to sleep peacefully through it all.

Incidentally, Miss Firth, who was a keen student of psychology and its powers of healing, mentions that all her affairs in life were chiefly concerned with the figure 7.

Later on she came in touch with a woman who had occult powers and who was a trained hypnotist. This woman had a very uncanny power over her, and at times, when under the woman's influence, she could actually feel her soul being drawn out of her body. At such times she experienced a narrowing of her field of vision, a sense of imminent darkness, and she struggled to get free. An inner voice, in definite articulation told her what to do in order to break loose from this undesirable 'spell.' She gained her freedom, but it took her three years to recover from the effects.

But she had touched unseen things and felt their power and she made up her mind that she would study this further. One day, without any warning, astral vision opened, and she had the experience of seeing the 'unseen' and of being nearly 'scared out of her wits; in consequence'. From the time she had this 'contact' her life completely changed. She often received warnings or 'premonitions' of happenings months before they actually occurred.

Miss Firth related a very strange dream which brought her definite illumination on the course she was destined regard to certain psychological problems for purposes of healing. In this dream she was confronted with the Master under whose guidance she was to serve. One received this almost Divine training through intuition and meditation. Especially through meditation much could be achieved. Through the latter she was able to ask certain questions and formulate the answers. During the three years she was gaining this knowledge of the occult she first of all obtained spiritual experience in dreams; after this came certain phenomena, and then she was invested with certain psychic faculties.

She afterwards became acquainted with a very marvellous man, who could perform wonderful things. She had seen the soul of this man leave his body and return to it again. While the soul was absent his body was quite light, and could easily be picked up.

In the course of her travels Miss Firth visited Glastonbury, which she discovered through personal experience to be a wonderful spiritual centre, and there she came closely in touch with the invisible world.

In her concluding remarks, Miss Firth said that those who desired to obtain a knowledge of the occult must strive to raise consciousness to a higher plane, at the same time bringing down the spiritual forces to a lower level. This achieved, they became real – apparent. But at all times a knowledge of occult powers must be safeguarded by a spiritual outlook.

Mrs. Isabel Scott proved a very charming hostess.

Appendix 4

'The Use of Imagination in Art, Science and Business' **By Mac Tyler,** *The Occult Review* **Vol. XLVIII No. 1 July 1928**

"Where there is no Vision, the people perish," and where there is no imagination, there can be no Vision comprehensible to the personal self, for it is the principal function of this much misunderstood and often mistakenly abused function to interpret the abstract truths cognised by the inner spiritual Being, expressing them in terms which can be understood by the personal and outer mind.

Imagination is thus the mediator between the inner and the outer selves of man; between the seen and the unseen; between those inner realities which can be spiritually apprehended, but never objectively proven, and those outer faculties which now, even as of old, seek ever for a tangible and objective sign.

Imagination is not in itself Vision, but it may be regarded as the sensitive plate by means of which Vision is made manifest; and its activities, when functioning rightly, may be described in the words of the Earth Spirit in Goethe's *Faust*:

> "It is thus at the roaring Loom of Time I ply,
> And weave for God the garment thou seest Him by."

Imagination is the vehicle of dream rather than the source thereof, being definitely a faculty of the personality; whereas for the source of dream and vision we must penetrate far beyond the *persona,* or "mask," to the innermost mysteries of Being itself.

Imagination and Intuition are often confused by those who have not experienced the latter in its true form. This is hardly surprising, as the difference between them is most subtle, and almost impossible to describe in objective terms. Perhaps one can come near to defining them by saying that when Imagination alone is functioning, there is always a sense of becoming, whereas true Intuition lifts us to realms of pure Being, unconditioned by time.

Imagination is therefore that focussing point where the powers of the personality are synthesised and uplifted to contact the realities of the Divine and (relatively) formless worlds, and to clothe those realities with the interpretative qualities of form. Consequently, it is at once the greatest asset and the greatest danger, both to the individual and to the race.

It is the seed of genius; it is also the seed of insanity; and unless it is ensouled by inner truth and controlled by well-balanced reason, it may become a psychological cancer of stupendous dimensions, gradually absorbing all other faculties into itself, until some acute form of *paranoia* or *dementia praecox* ensues.

In the World of Art, the uses of Imagination are so manifest as to need little emphasis or elaboration, but in the World of Business it is often despised, and its eminently practical value ignored.

It can never be sufficiently emphasised that the only satisfactory basis of business enterprise is an adequate appreciation of human values. This depends upon what Algernon Blackwood calls the faculty of "inside sight," feeling with people to the point of understanding their needs and cravings from the inside, even as they themselves understand them; and for this process Imagination is absolutely essential.

Blackwood's *Prisoner in Fairyland* is a perfect expression of spiritual truth intuitionally apprehended and embodied in the most delicately beautiful imaginative form.

Only this image-building faculty of the mind can relate and interpret to the personality that which the sensitive inner Being registers of another's pain or need, and thus enable us to put ourselves mentally and consciously in the other person's place, to view his circumstances from his own standpoint, and to share his pain and limitation by the identification of our consciousness with his.

Such a mental process is preliminary to all true healing, either social or individual, and only by a wide and generous application of this principle can we hope to heal the terrible wounds which are poisoning social and business life to-day.

If Capital and Labour would but strive to feel with each other, instead of striving continuously to outdo each other, many of our sorest social problems would automatically find solution, for if we truly felt the need and suffering of others as though it were our own, we should not rest, we could not rest, until that suffering had been alleviated, that need supplied.

It is because business people as a class are sadly neglectful in applying imaginative faculty (while many are actually deficient in that respect) that they are unable to translate in terms comprehensible to the personal self those realities which their inner Beings apprehend; and so, for lack of a bridge between the higher and lower selves, or between the inner and the outer, they endure existences of terrible and unnecessary psychological limitation, producing often unintentional and sometimes almost incredible brutality in human relationships, whether of the business or social world.

Many well-meaning people would be horrified beyond measure could they see and understand the cruelties of which, owing to deficiency of imaginative faculty and sympathetic insight, they are sometimes guilty. The great majority of people do not deliberately desire to give pain, and the suffering they inflict is an unconscious by-product of the self-preservation instinct, often arising from fear, which, as Galsworthy truly said, "is the black godmother of all damnable things."

On the other hand, there are cases in which, although the imaginative faculty may be well developed, it is applied in a purely negative way. In curative psychological work one often comes across such instances. In many such cases the patient's imagination is used only negatively, to enable its possessor to evade unpleasant responsibilities; or to plan for personal advancement, wholly regardless of other people's claims and their possible detriment; or sometimes even to create for its possessor some convenient ailment which shall exempt the patient from unpleasant duties, procuring him sympathetic indulgence and unremitting attention from the other members of the family circle.

Such negative and destructive forms of imaginative activity have brought into much disrepute an invaluable faculty which, rightly used, should be essentially and creatively altruistic in function, widening our sympathies, breaking down the artificial barriers of caste and clan and creed, and enabling us to meet all men and women on equal terms of frank comradeship and brotherliness.

In the world of Science, as in the world of Art, this imaginative faculty is given a far more honoured place than in the world of Business; for the scientist knows that it is the pioneering faculty by the help of which all the most brilliant scientific attainments have been achieved.

The scientist checks and weighs its promptings with the utmost care, but he rarely neglects to take it into consideration as the business man so often does, and he rarely permits it to rule him entirely as the artist so often does.

The artist's imaginative faculty is frequently in need of training and discipline, for unless it is balanced by clear reason, it is apt to distort the spiritual truths it strives to express, instead of embodying them in beautiful and helpful form. But a force misdirected is of greater evolutionary value than a force crippled, distorted, crushed almost out of existence. The misdirection is only a matter for mental education; but the healing of a withered and starved imagination is a process requiring infinitely deeper knowledge and more gradual, more far-reaching modes of service, operating not from the mental but from the spiritual plane.

Where we cannot achieve counsels of perfection in our educational system, it would be infinitely wiser to permit some measure of over-development to a child's imagination, rather than to check or thwart it. Little permanent harm will result if the imaginative faculty is carefully fed on beauty of truth, nature, art, and brotherhood, even though its functions may seem for a time to be somewhat over-emphasised. Beauty may be defined as truth expressed graciously, therefore right training in the appreciation of beauty will automatically produce an innate sense of balance. True balance must always be the result of inner poise rather than of outer criticism and correction. The expression of outer criticism it often a tacit admission of our own failure to render inner sustenance to the one we criticise. All true growth and healing is from within outwards; therefore those who would minister to another's psychological need must learn to do so from the innermost sphere where all life is realised as one in essence, though manifesting outwardly in diversity of myriad forms.

Comparatively few of us are able to realise this truth continuously as an abstract fact, but aided by Imagination on the personal plane and by Intuition on the spiritual plane, and working in terms of the Law of Correspondences, we may realise it by means of analogies, and so attain in Art, Science and Business the only sound basis of practical universal brotherhood.

The true evolutionary purpose of Imagination is to enable the Personality to quarry from the dull uninspiring grind of everyday life, material which shall be transformed by the alchemic action of spiritual potencies into a Universal Temple, dedicated to the glory of that sublime Indwelling Divinity, which, though sometimes latent and wholly hidden, is nevertheless imminent in every unit of Humanity.

Appendix 5

Aleister Crowley's own account of his life, published in three parts in The Weekly Despatch, 18 June–2 July 1933

Part 1: 'The Worst Man in the World'

If there is one subject I detest it is Aleister Crowley. On the other hand, there's no mystery about it. So, if anybody is interested, here goes!

I have been shot at with broad arrows. They have called me the 'worst man in the world.' They have accused me of doing everything from murdering women and throwing their bodies into the Seine to drug peddling. Some well-known journalists delighted in attacking me in print. James Douglas described me as 'a monster of wickedness.' Horatio Bottomley branded me as a 'dirty degenerate' cannibal – everything he could think of.

Some have been more precise. In a book I picked up recently the author told of how I murdered cats with terrible ritual in Sicily. Certain irresponsible newspapers accused me of having murdered my secretary! The value of all this nonsense is somewhat discounted by the fact that I am back in England after wandering over most of the world, and go my way without interference. No charge of any sort ever been preferred against me.

Legend says that my dossier at Scotland Yard fills a whole room. There is a story that Lord Byng, when he took over, saw a wing of the building particularly vast and quite unusually guarded exclaimed: "What's that?" "The files about Aleister Crowley." "Goodness gracious me!" "Of course, we haven't got the last month's stuff in yet. A bit congested." "Here, this has to stop! We can't put up new buildings every few weeks. Close the record!"

Nobody stops to look at me in the street. My appearance is, I suppose, of a simple country gentleman up in town for a week-end. All my notoriety arises from the fact that I am a magician. I AM THE MASTER

THERION. Practically my whole life has been spent in the study of magic. Foolish people say that I am a Black Magician, that I am in the habit of celebrating the Black Mass and the Witches Sabbath, that I eat new-born babes and explore the sky on a broomstick. They say that Satan is my master and that I am his faithful agent.

But I am a white magician, not a black one. I belong to a secret Order which has representatives all over the world; we are all working for the good of humanity, not for its downfall.

Let me say here that it is impossible for a magician to be a man of bad character. He cares nothing for conventions, but he needs the sternest virtues. His powers are limited by himself. The man, who having practised strange rites, becomes a drunkard or a drug-fiend, a failure as a magician. He has lost his grip.

That brings me to what is magic. The ordinary man is inclined to laugh at the word. He says that it is a phantom of the morbid and ignorant minds of ancient and the Middle Ages. Yet he is superstitious enough to believe in signs and omens, in astrologers and palmists, who claim to read destiny in stars and hands.

If an Englishman of a generation or two ago could have been shown a little black box and told that if he turned a knob the President of the United States would talk to him, he would have laughed at the idea. If one could have convinced him that the voice was actually that of the President that Englishman would have been forced to the conclusion that the black box was magical. And yet we know now that the feat is quite possible and that the box is only that kind of magic now revealed to the profane as 'radio.'

What is magic to-day is science to-morrow. The Hindus 'worship Idols.' Yes? But what exactly do they mean by that? As I myself have observed, they get very interesting results from their 'worship.' We, the enlightened West, say that their worship is ignorant superstition and the results coincidence. But are we not in the position of our mythical Englishman listening to the noise from the black box?

In my textbook 'Theory and Practice of Magick' will be found the definition of the word magic, or magick, as I prefer to spell it, to distinguish the real from the false. It is 'the science and art of causing change to occur in accordance with the will. We magicians are men of science, who by the practice of our craft keep just ahead of popular understanding and blackguarded all our lives.

After we are dead – sometimes centuries after – the world catches up, and discovers that we were benefactors and not villains. I am writing these articles as an explanation of magic. Unfortunately, my name is universally identified with the subject, so I fear I must drag myself into the arena. Let me condense my personal history into a few paragraphs.

I was born in Leamington. Warwickshire, on October 12, 1875, the son of Edward Crowley, who was a colleague of John Nelson Darby the founder of Plymouth Brethren. At birth I had three of the distinguishing marks of a Buddha. I was tongue-tied, I had a characteristic membrane which necessitated an operation, and over the centre of my heart I had four hairs curling from left to right in the exact form of a Swastika.

At school I had passions for poetry and chemistry. I had an instinct for chess; experience rapidly proved my ability. I never lost to anyone until – at Cambridge – I met H. E. Atkins, seven years running amateur champion of Britain. It was at Cambridge that I perceived the futility of worldly ambitions. I had wanted to be a poet and to attain the greatest success in the Diplomatic Service, for which the late Lord Salisbury had intended me.

Suddenly the ordinary ambitions of life seemed empty and worthless. Time crumbles all; I must find durable material for building. I sought desperately for help, for light. I raided every library and bookshop in the University. One book told me of a secret community of saints in possession of every spiritual grace, of the keys of the treasure of Nature. The members of this church lived their secret life of sanctity in the world, radiating light and love on all those that came within their scope.

The sublimity of the idea enthralled me; it satisfied my craving for romance and poetry. I determined with my whole heart to make myself worthy to attract the notice of this mysterious brotherhood. Then one of the first principles of magic was revealed to me. It is sufficient to will with all one's might that which one wills. You who read this – whatever you will you can do. It is only a question of commanding the means.

The first proof that I had of this miracle working capacity which is latent in every man was this: even before I had issued the call for guidance there was a man at my side to answer it.

But this first call: 1898 in a Bierhalle under the shadow of the Matterhorn I met an alchemist. He is one of the best-known technical chemists in London. One of his scientific feats was the 'fixing' of mercury (i.e. the making of it solid at ordinary temperatures) and he had done this by the despised alchemical processes of the Middle Ages.

He was a member of the Hermetic Order of the Golden Dawn, fraudulent imitations of which have created so much scandal in later years. Through his good offices I was initiated into the Order in November, 1898.

I realised that I had found the key to illimitable knowledge and power, that I had started the path which enables a man to transcend all the inflictions and disappointments of life. The Path! I did not guess that it would lead me through all the most obscure and dangerous lands upon this planet, and to cost me £100.000 for a one-way ticket.

The Path! One of the final secrets, listen, is this. Not even the inexpressible glory and rapture of the goal, but the Path itself, with all its dangers, hardships and distress, is the reward worthwhile!

The initiation ceremony was impressive. I was handed over by my sponsors at the door of a secret temple (even today I must not reveal its whereabouts) by the Kerux or Herald; a man in a golden robe with a drawn sword.

He conducted me through the first of the Great Pylons. After being blindfolded and bound, purified by being sprinkled with water and consecrated by fire. I was led into semi-darkness thick with fumes of incense.

I was made to kneel before an altar and repeat a formidable oath of fidelity, of secrecy and of abstinence from any kind of conduct which might impair my powers of self control. The hoodwink was removed from my eyes at a throne set up in darkness in the west. Here I was confronted by a black-hooded officer representative of the god Horus. He gave me my first injunction: 'Fear is failure and the forerunner of failure. Be thou therefore without fear, for in the heart of the coward virtue abideth not. Thou hest known me. Pass thou on.'

The hoodwink was removed also when I arrived at the throne in the east, where the officer representing the god Osiris gave me another injunction – that the path of attainment lies through the knowledge and use of perfect balance, justice, righteousness, and truth.

Finally I was unbound and bidden to take my place in the north, the place of greatest darkness, to show that I had taken only the first step in a long and difficult road.

All this ritual may strike the reader as being unnecessary. But its purpose is to stamp the injunctions indelibly on the memory – more upon deeper parts of the spiritual being of man than the superficial strata of the conscious mind. I am forbidden to mention the names of those who initiated me, but among them were some of the most distinguished men and women in the Empire in literature, art, politics, the theatre, diplomacy, and the army.

I was then a neophyte – a new being born into a new world. I have never gone back to the old world of the gross deceptions and illusions of matter as the senses describe it. Those who become magicians can travel in the astral plane, visiting distant places while the body still stays at home. They have prepared and proved an elixir of life; they are often seen surrounded with an aura of light.

I have myself tested all these claims and find them true. There is no limit to the possibilities of an attainment. But these are only superficial things. Magic transcends space and time. All things are possible to an adept, but the virtue of his knowledge and power would depart if he used them for selfish ends or personal gain. In fact the words 'selfish' and 'personal' cease to mean anything to the initiate. He develops himself, and finds himself by losing his old limited self in all that is: for 'eyerything that lives is holy.'

Part 2: I Make Myself Invisible

After my initiation I seemed to myself like a savage who happens to wander into a factory of high explosives. I had to learn the laws of life all over again from the beginning. I always think of Mr Wells's 'First Men in the Moon.' How to act when the fundamental conditions of life are changed? The danger of making fatal mistakes is always present.

A necessary part of the practice of magic is the Invocation of Divine and angelic beings and the evocation of blind forces, some of which are considered "evil" by the vulgar. Of course there are forces which are definitely malicious. It is never necessary for a magician to deal with them, except as a bacteriologist studies disease germs, to find out their nature and subdue them.

By 1899 I had gone through seven stages of initiation. These constituted me an Adept, but accidents were still happening to me. I constructed a private temple in a flat in Chancery Lane. It was a hall of mirrors, the function of which was to concentrate the invoked forces. It contained an altar of acacia topped with gold and certain secret symbols and regalia of the Order.

One night, after a ceremony in which a well-known analytical chemist was my leader, I locked the door and went out with him to a meal. When we returned the door was wide open, though the lock had not been forced, and the whole contents of the temple had been thrown about and lay in the wildest confusion. Then the fun began. We saw – and my teacher was able to identify hundreds of shapes, weird "half-formed faces" which were thronging the room, marching in fantastic dance about its confines. These were definitely malicious forces, demons, which one had to study and conqueror.

Later, when I was transferring my apparatus to my house in Scotland. I employed two workmen to remove the mirrors. As they were working they were suddenly overcome, knocked-out by unseen assailants. It took several hours to revive them. People passing the doorway suddenly fell down in fits. That flat remained without a tenant for years after I had left it. All this was because I had not enough experience to control the forces. It was at the direction of the head of the Order that I then went to Scotland to my manor house of Boleskine, which is two or three miles from the Falls of Foyers.

My subsidiary object – the principal aim is too sacred to discuss – put into simple language, was to gain control over the 'four great princes' of the evil of the world. According to the rules of magic, I built a terrace with a northern aspect and carted river-sand to it. I worked in the breakfast-room at making the talismans which were necessary to my purpose. The sun was streaming into the room, but in vain; there was a darkness which could be felt. The demons, evil forces, had congregated round me so thickly that they were shutting off the light. It was a comforting situation. There could be no more doubt of the efficiency of the operation.

But I went on with my work, even though I had to light a lamp – with the sun shining brightly outside. The demons collected, also in the lodge which I had built on the terrace. They were still vague shapes, half-seen faces. I got used to them. They had curious effects on the neighbourhood. Part of the main road from Inverness to Fort Augustus ran through my estate. Soon superstitions about the road made the natives avoid it. People refused to use it after nightfall.

Even the tough, hard-drinking workmen from Glasgow who were employed at Foyers would go a long way round to avoid that uncanny road. The forces had other and worse effects.

An employee (who had not touched alcohol for 20 years) suddenly got drunk and tried to murder his wife and children. This was one of many similar cases. One summer more than half my pack of bloodhounds died. My servants were always getting ill. One of the men I employed to lay down putting-greens went insane and tried to murder my wife. I had realised, by time, that my path to power was to be immensely difficult and fraught with danger. But I did not look back.

I began my pilgrimage to far-distant countries. Mexico was the first. I was sent there by the head of the Order to Consecrate a priest to serve the 'Lamp of the Invisible Light.' In Mexico, too, I made my first experiments in acquiring invisibility. By invoking the God of Silence, Harpocrates, by the proper ritual in front of a mirror. It gradually got to the stage where my reflection began to flicker like the images of one of the old-fashioned cinemas. It never disappeared completely. In fact, that experiment showed me that I was on the wrong track. Success lay not in an optical disappearance. but in the power of fascination. 'Having eyes, they see not.' However that may be. I was able to walk out in a scarlet-and-gold robe with a jewelled crown on my head without attracting any attention. They could not see me.

This was the beginning of an art which stood me in good stead in Calcutta years later. While I was walking through the native quarter at night I was set upon by robbers. When I saw a knife flash I thought it was beyond a joke; pinioned though I was, I managed to fire my revolver. Hundreds of natives aroused by the report rushed out to seek me, but I was able to walk unperceived through the midst of them, and make my escape.

My travels took me to Ceylon, where I devoted myself to Yoga. I took a bungalow at Kandy and was steered through the beginnings of the art. Yoga may be taught in eight words. 'Sit still. Stop thinking! Shut up! Get out!' It is the learning that is difficult. My success with Yoga was so great that it became dangerous. For my own good I left it alone for two years, departing from Ceylon and going to India. A curious thing happened on occasion. At Madura I went into a temple and sacrificed a goat. Soon after I completely cut off my trail by a sea voyage – a great storm was raging, and I was the only person to board the ship.

Some time afterwards I returned to India and visited some friends, who knew nothing about my activities in Calcutta. They told me that their servants were excited about a queer tale that I had sacrificed a goat at Madura, the most sacred city of South India. How had the natives obtained that information? They had done it by 'native telegraph.' I then went to Egypt, and – to my intense surprise – was summoned by the secret chiefs of the Order. I was commanded to return to England, there to reconstruct the system of organisation, as the outer form of the Order had broken up through the fall of its chief ambassador to the world 'without the veil,' and to put the secrets in writing.

I accordingly condensed and published knowledge in a periodical called 'The Equinox.' Headquarters at the time was a studio in Victoria Street. There in our spare time we began to celebrate the rites of Eleusis. Some of these rites were often attended with strange results. On several occasions we saw and felt a stranger among us, but when the lights were turned higher there was no one there. Our ceremonies had caused a being to take human form and be seen among us. The success of these private rituals induced me to take the Caxton Hall for seven performances, which were open to the public. Bottomley attacked the rituals as obscene and blasphemous. He was merely reflecting in print the depravity of his own mind.

A girl played the violin during the rites. She was a good violinist, but under the influence of the ceremonies she was more; she played sublimely, like a supreme virtuoso, in the magical invocations directed upon her. During one ceremony in July 1909, in the Victoria Street studio, we invoked Bartzabel, the spirit of Mars. One of those present was a man of importance in the Admiralty, a commander whose name is too well known to mention. He asked the spirit, which had been invoked in a specially purified and consecrated man. if "nation would ever rise against nation." Bartzabel answered that it would. Questioned further, the spirit said that war would break out within five years, and that the nations which would be smashed would be Turkey and Germany.

Within a fortnight of the end of those five years the Great War broke out. The naval man was an Adept of the Order, and he played a big part in the struggle. Whenever the affairs of the world reach a critical stage the Adepts always have someone behind the scenes. Rudoph Steiner, the man who was responsible for the defeat of Germany, was Grand Master of the O.T.O. in Austria, a semi-masonic order of which I was the Grand Master in England.

Steiner broke away from the Order, because he became terrified at one of the ordeals he had to go through. He was thus cut off from the true magic, but he became secret adviser to Von Moltke. Steiner's direction resulted in Von Moltke's failing to take Paris when it was within his grasp, and that mistake cost Germany the whole war. Steiner had proved his inability to become a great magician and he was deceived by treacherous powers into defeating his country.

Part 3: Black Magic is Not a Myth

Black Magic is not a myth. It is a totally unscientific and emotional form of magic, but it does get results – of an extremely temporary nature. The recoil upon those who practise it is terrific. It is like looking for an escape of gas with a lighted candle. As far as the search goes, there is little fear of failure!

To practise black magic you have to violate every principle of science, decency and intelligence. You must be obsessed with an insane idea of the importance of the petty object of your wretched and selfish desires.

I have been accused of being a 'black magician.' No more foolish statement was ever made about me. I despise the thing to such an extent that I can hardly believe in the existence of people so debased and idiotic as to practise it.

In Paris, and even in London, there are misguided people who are abusing their priceless spiritual gifts to obtain petty and temporary advantages through these practices.

The 'Black Mass' is a totally different matter. I could not celebrate it if I wanted to, for I am not a consecrated priest of the Christian Church. The celebrant must be a priest, for the whole idea of the practice is to profane the Sacrament of the Eucharist. Therefore you must believe in the truth of the cult and the efficacy of its ritual.

A renegade priest gathers about him a congregation of sensation-hunters and religious fanatics: then only can the ceremonies of profanation be of extended black magical effect. But even in his robes there is some sinister change, a perversion of their symbolic sanctity. There are many ways of abusing this Sacrament. One of the best known of which is the 'Mass of the Saint Sécaire,' the purpose of which is to cause an enemy to wither away. At this 'mass' always held in some sacred place, preferably in a disused chapel, at midnight, the priest appears in canonical robes. But even in his robes there is some sinister change, a perversion of their symbolic sanctity.

There is an altar, but the candles are of black wax. The crucifix is fixed with the head downward. The clerk to the priest is a woman and her dress, although it seems to be a church garment, is more like a costume in a prurient revue. It was altered to make it indecent. The ceremony is a parody of the orthodox mass, with blasphemous interpolations. The priest must be careful, however to consecrate the host in the orthodox manner. The wine has been adulterated with magical drugs like deadly nightshade and vervain but the priest must convert it into the blood of Christ.

The dreadful basis of the Mass is that the bread and the wine have imprisoned the Deity. Then they are subjected to terrible profanations. This is supposed to release the powers of evil and bring them into alliance. (It is rather the case of the mouse trying to make a friend of the cat!) In the congregational form of the Black Mass the priest, having finished his abominations these are, quite frankly, indescribable – scatters the fragments, the possession of which, they believe, will allow them to work their petty and malicious designs.

My most memorable personal experience of the effects of black magic occurred when I was living to Scotland. The machinations of a degraded and outcast member of the Order caused my hounds to die and my servants to become ill. The struggle lasted until the recoil of the current of hatred caused the luckless sorcerer to collapse. The explanation of its effects is that, if you believe passionately enough in your will to do something, then power to achieve it will accrue to you. My enemies say that the celebration of the 'Black Mass' was one of the most innocuous of my activities in Sicily and in France. 'Why was he thrown out of both those countries?' they ask.

The explanation of why I left is quite simple and unsensational. I took a villa at Cefalù in Sicily for work and play. We began the day with family prayers, we occasionally celebrated a semi-religious ceremony known as the Gnostic Mass.

Several people who were my guests at the 'abbey' made imaginative copy out of their visits. Then the Fascists came to power and some foreign newspaper correspondents were asked to leave. And so was I. There was no rough turning out. I was treated with the greatest courtesy.

The reason I left Paris was that the authorities refused to renew my *carte d'identite*. No charge was made against me; and no explanation given. Somebody I had quarrelled with had gone to the authorities and succeeded in making them think that something was wrong.

Spiritualism – more correctly, spiritism – is not a form of Black Magic. Through their mediums the spiritists sometimes get hold of disintegrated pieces of a man or woman who has died recently. The apparatus has lost its guiding control, the spiritual side of a man and it can be – and often is – taken by elemental spirits of evil and turned to any base use. Spiritists are playing with malicious forces.

Witchcraft is a more or less solitary form of black magic. By working herself into a diabolic ecstasy the witch can achieve success in her schemes. She is willing to sacrifice her first-born, a usual price demanded by the demon, or sell her soul. And all what for what? To stop her neighbour's cows from giving milk; to send a surly enemy to a sick bed. The effect is completely ridiculous compared with the waste of spiritual forces required to produce it.

The true magician is above spite or venom. He tries to bring about the results for which he is working, not by sudden and disruptive interference with the existing order of things but by slow natural processes. In theory there is no limit to the power of magic. A magician is like a mathematician; he has complete control of the symbols as long as he keeps to the rules.

I have prepared the elixir of life, that magical draught which gives eternal youth. Like the touch of Midas, it is not an unmixed blessing. I made it first when I was forty. It was done hastily and with imperfect knowledge. I took seven doses – as the first two or three had no apparent effect – the consequences were extremely violent. One day, without warning, I woke up to find that I had lost all my maturity. Became mentally and physically a stupid stripling. The only thing I could think of doing was to cut down trees. I was living in a cottage in New Hampshire; for fifteen hours a day I toiled at felling trees. I worked like a madman. No feat of strength was too great for me.

These fantastic physical powers lasted about two months, and were followed by reaction. For half a year I was in a state of lassitude. I had been playing with a dangerous recipe. Six years later I experimented again with the elixir, taking precautions to avoid such drastic results. The result was that at 47 I was as powerful an athlete as any man of 30. I still retain much of the good effect of this experiment. My intellectual activity has not only been conserved but intensified, and I am still enjoying perfect health and energy.

Bibliography

Alison, Archibald, *Principles of the Criminal Law of Scotland* (Edinburgh, 1832)

Byrne, Francis, *Irish Kings and High Kings* (Batsford, 1973)

Calder-Marshall, Arthur, *The Magic of My Youth* (Hart-Davis, 1951)

Cammell, Charles Richard, *Aleister Crowley The Man: The Mage: The Poet* (Richards, 1951)

Campbell, Reverend John Gregorson, *Superstitions of the Highlands and Islands of Scotland* (MacLehose, 1900)

Colquhoun, Ithell, *The Living Stones: Cornwall* (Owen, 1957)

Colquhoun, Ithell, Sword of Wisdom: MacGregor Mathers and the Golden Dawn (Spearman, 1975)

Crowley, Aleister, *The Confessions of Aleister Crowley: An Autohagiography* (Cape, 1969)

Crowley, Aleister, *Magick in Theory and Practice* (Privately Published, 1929)

Dearden, Dr Harold, *Devilish but True: The Doctor Looks at Spiritualism* (Hutchinson, 1936)

Doyle, Sir Arthur Conan et al, *My Religion* (Hutchinson, 1975)

Doyle, Sir Arthur Conan, *The Case for Spirit Photography* (Hodder, 1922)

Doyle, Sir Arthur Conan, *The Coming of the Fairies* (Hodder, 1922)

Fortune, Dion, *Practical Occultism* (Thoth, 2002)

Fortune, Dion, *Psychic Self-Defence: A Study in Occult Pathology and Criminality* (Rider, 1930)

Fortune, Dion, *The Secrets of Dr Taverner* (Douglas, 1926)

Fuller, Jean Overton, *The Magical Dilemma of Victor Neuburg* (Revised Edition) (Mandrake, 1990)

Hardy, Robin and Shaffer, Anthony, *The Wicker Man* (Pan, 2000)

Hamnett, Nina, *The Laughing Torso* (Constable, 1932)

Heywood Hadfield, P., *With an Orient Liner through the Fjords of Norway* (London Stereoscopic, 1922)

Hodson, Geoffrey, *Fairies at Work and Play* (Theosophical, 1925)

Hutton, Ronald, *The Triumph of the Moon: A History of Modern Pagan Witchcraft* (Oxford, 1999)

Johnson, Dr Samuel, *A Journey to the Western Isles of Scotland* (Strahan and Cadell, 1775)

Jones, Richard Glyn, *The Black Magic Murders* (Xanadu, 1988)

Küntz, Darcy (ed.), *The Battle of Blythe Road: A Golden Dawn Affair* (Holmes, 2000)

Lane, Brian, *The Murder Guide* (Robinson, 1991)

Laver, James, *Museum Piece* (Deutsch, 1963)

MacArthur, E. Mairi, *Columba's Island* (Edinburgh University Press, 1995)

Macdonald, *Criminal Law of Scotland* (Green, 1948)

MacGregor, Alasdair Alpin, *The Ghost Book* (Hale, 1955)

MacLeod, Fiona (William Sharp), *The Divine Adventure: Iona* (Heinemann, 1910)

MacLeod, Fiona (William Sharp), *The Dominion of Dreams* (Constable, 1909)

MacLeod, Fiona (William Sharp), *The Immortal Hour* (Birmingham School of Printing, 1939)

May, Betty, *Tiger Woman* (Duckworth, 1929)

Neuburg, Victor B,. *The Green Garland* (Young Cambridge, 1908)

Oakley, Ben, *Death on Iona* (Twelvetrees, 2023)

Oddie, Ingleby, *Inquest: A Coroner Looks Back* (Hutchinson, 1941)
Pinner, David, *Ritual* (New Authors, 1967)
Richardson, Alan, *The Magical Life of Dion Fortune* (Aquarian, 1991)
Symonds, John, *The Great Beast* (Rider, 1951)
Thompson, Frances, *The Supernatural Highlands* (Robert Hale, 1976)
Traill, Henry Duf, *From Cairo to the Soudan Frontier* (Lane, 1896)
Whittington-Egan, Molly, *Classic Scottish Murder Stories* (Wilson, 1999)
Wilson, Richard, *Scotland's Unsolved Mysteries*, (Hale, Revised Edition, 1995)

Newspapers and guidebooks are annotated in the text.

Acknowledgements

The author would like to record his personal thanks to the following for their help and encouragement with this book and my research in this field over the years:

The British Library, The National Archives, National Library of Scotland, United Grand Lodge of England Museum of Freemasonry, The Mull Museum, Argyll and Bute Council, Bishop's Stortford Museum, Essex Record Office, Mintlyn Crematorium, Stewart P. Evans, Rob Clack, Delianne Forget, Michelle Bullivant, Liz Cormell, Kerry Freeman, Melita Morgan, Martin Faulks, my much-missed friend the late Andrew Selwyn-Crome, my commissioning editor and all the editorial and design team at Pen & Sword, the music of Ralph Vaughan Williams, especially *Fantasia on a Theme by Thomas Tallis*, played by The BBC Symphony Orchestra conducted by Andrew Davis at Gloucester Cathedral where the piece was originally played and conducted for the first time by its composer in 1910. This music has helped me through some of the very dark aspects of the research for this book, and last but by no means least, I give my sincere thanks to my ever-loving family.

Dear Reader,

We hope you have enjoyed this book, but why not share your views on social media? You can also follow our pages to see more about our other products: facebook.com/penandswordbooks or follow us on X @penswordbooks

You can also view our products at www.pen-and-sword.co.uk (UK and ROW) or www.penandswordbooks.com (North America).

To keep up to date with our latest releases and online catalogues, please sign up to our newsletter at: www.pen-and-sword.co.uk/newsletter

If you would like a printed catalogue with our latest books, then please email: enquiries@pen-and-sword.co.uk or telephone: 01226 734555 (UK and ROW) or email: uspen-and-sword@casematepublishers.com or telephone: (610) 853-9131 (North America).

We respect your privacy and we will only use personal information to send you information about our products.

Thank you!